HEALING FROM THE HEART

THE INHERENT POWER
TO HEAL FROM WITHIN

Judith S. Moore, D.O.

Moore Heart Enterprises

Healing from the Heart
By Judith S. Moore, D.O.

For further information, contact the author at:

Moore Heart Enterprises
c/o Vitality House Publishing
1675 North Freedom Boulevard, #11-C
Provo, Utah 84604-2570
1-800-748-5100
Fax: 1-801-373-3426
e-mail: vitalityhouse@freedommedcenter.com

Book design by The Floating Gallery:
331 West 57th Street, #465, New York, NY 10019
(212) 399-1961 www.thefloatinggallery.com

PRINTED IN THE UNITED STATES OF AMERICA

Moore, Judith S.
Healing from the Heart

1. Author 2. Title
Library of Congress Catalog Card Number: 2001127018
ISBN 0-9715287-0-5 Hardcover

Healing from the Heart is an inspirational story full of insights into why people fail to heal. By using knowledge discovered in the field of psychoneuroimmunology, the concepts contained in this book are revolutionizing the way the medical world views healing in both physical and emotional illnesses. The principles are taught in simple, delightful tales so that they are easy to understand. By learning these principles each individual can discover the thoughts, emotions and beliefs that may be holding back their own healing. By applying each principle to their lives through the guided imagery on the CDs, individuals can empower their hearts to assist in the healing process, dramatically improving their ability to heal and enhancing their rate of healing. Many who have lost hope because of their illness will find their life revitalized through the visualization processes found in this book.

ABOUT THE AUTHOR

Dr. Judith S. Moore is a board-certified Osteopathic Family Practice Physician practicing in Provo, Utah. She specializes in "difficult-to-treat" cases by integrating both western and alternative medicine to allow healing in all levels of the body. She co-authored Marie Osmond's book, *Behind the Smile: My Journey Out of Postpartum Depression*, describing the way she assisted Marie in her healing. She is currently involved in starting a new medical school that would teach medical students these principles through integrating them into their basic courses. She is also planning a hospital where patients may be treated wholistically with integrative medicine. Dr. Moore is founder and chairman of the Foundation for the Advancement of Integrative Medicine, which has the purpose of raising money for these purposes. She is donating a percentage of the proceeds of this book to this foundation.

For further information on this book or other books published by Vitality House, or to order more copies, contact:

Moore Heart Enterprises
c/o Vitality House Publishing
1675 North Freedom Boulevard, #11-C
Provo, Utah 84604-2570
1-800-748-5100
Fax: 1-801-373-3426
e-mail: vitalityhouse@freedommedcenter.com

Table of Contents

ACKNOWLEDGEMENTS

I appreciate those who put great time and effort into making this book the quality that it is: Doug Moore, my husband, for his creative heart; Sharon Brown, my sister, and Marcia Wilkie for their honest and thoughtful editing; Nancy Macfarlane for proofreading and always lifting me with encouraging words; Larry and Joel at The Floating Gallery for their expertise and patience; and Marie Osmond for giving me a voice and for taking time out of her incredibly busy life to write the foreword and support my work. I appreciate the assistance of those who put their spirits into the CD to make it a healing work of art: Lisa Edwards, director and producer; Robin Hancock, pianist extraordinaire; Elizabeth Deters, musical genius and violinist; the comforting voice of Carolyn Smith; and the expertise of Darin Rhodes at Rosewood Recording Studio.

I appreciate those who contributed to and shaped my life: my parents, Jesse and Helen Stay, who taught me about God and led me to believe I can do anything, and especially my mother's wonderful storytelling; Tanis Hase, Stephen Thornburg, D.O., and Viola Frymann, D.O., my inspiring teachers; Kent and Linda Pendleton and Hans and Sally Berger for teaching me how to connect with the great healer within; Brian Conn and Bernie Dorhmann for inspiring me to write; my children, Jason, Tonya, Tina, Tom, Monica and Shane, for being my greatest teachers and allowing me to be who I am; my dear husband Doug who supports my work wholeheartedly and is always there to lean on; and especially my loving Father, my God, who provided His Son to show me that with God, nothing is impossible.

FOREWORD

Recently I was carrying my little boy down the concrete steps of an office building following an appointment at the dentist. He had been both shy and nervous about this new experience, but now, in my arms, he was proud of his "big boy" behavior after finding out it wasn't so bad. Trying to balance a 35-pound toddler and a carryall bag that nearly weighs the same (many mothers know what I'm talking about) is never easy, even on level ground.

Still, being the mother of seven, I've given up on "easy" and only concern myself with the most efficient way to get from point A to point B, because at point B is another child waiting to be picked up from dance class, volleyball, or a friend's house. I've maneuvered down a flight of steps with 50 or 60 extra pounds in my arms and single strap sandals on my feet on many, many occasions.

This time, however, with one misplaced step, I found myself airborne, the top of the staircase being my take-off point. If the normal first instinct is to put your hands out to break a fall, I bypassed it instantly to protect my son. I closed my arms around his back, my hand covering his head and tried to shift my body so he would land on me and not me on him. What I managed to do was get my legs back under me, and landed on my shins at the bottom of the stairs, child still protected in arms.

My adrenaline was flooding through every cell and my heart was pounding by the time I came to a complete stop. I expected my son to cry out in fear, but he seemed completely unaffected by the whole fall. In fact, he giggled, prying my arms from his torso, and said: "Mommy, you're dec-o-lass." (The four-year-old pronunciation of "ridiculous.")

Once I knew he was fine, I gathered up the twenty or so things that had spilled from the bag and got to my feet. I could see my shin was bleeding, but I was more concerned with the next stop in my schedule, and I got out my keys and hurried us across the parking lot.

It wasn't until we were in the car that I really began to feel the injury on my leg. The concrete had literally dug a trench seven inches long down my shin and the whole area was searing with pain in a matter of seconds.

I made sure to squeeze into the schedule a stop at Dr. Judith Moore's office. She took a look at my leg and ordered me into a room for a cleanup treatment. After washing the wound, dressing it, and giving me a dose of homeopathic medicine, she told me to go home and rest. As busy as I was, I've learned over the course of the last year and a half, while being treated by Dr. Moore for Postpartum Depression, to give attention to her advice.

I headed home to find myself in tears, not from the injury, but from the vulnerable emotions and memories that came to the surface from taking an unpredictable spill over which I had little control. Before I met Dr. Moore, I might have pushed these feelings away as silly or self-indulgent. I don't do that anymore. It takes too large of a toll on me in the long run. In my own life, everything that I've pushed away or ignored has never really disappeared. It's only re-surfaced at a different time and circumstance.

I've come to understand what amazing vehicles our bodies truly are. They know how to naturally prioritize. For example, in my fall down the stairs, my system somehow knew that I had to protect my baby first. My adrenaline surge probably gave me the strength to hang onto him and my instincts told me it was better to land on my shins than let my head hit the ground. I felt no extreme pain in my leg until I had us both to safety. Then, my body sent the signal to my brain that I had an injury that needed attention. After the wound was given attention, my emotions told me that I needed to process the feelings that came from such an unexpected and scary turn of events.

Dr. Moore has made her life's work a dedication to total health care: the body, the mind and the heart. Her prescriptions are much more than a pill and a bandage. She examines the connection between the mind, the heart and the health of her patients. She looks at the "why" of a person's illness, and not just the "how to get rid of the symptoms." Under her care, I've discovered for myself what could be the basis of my own physical strengths and weaknesses. In this book, through story and visualizations, Dr. Moore opens the channels to the possible underlying causes of illness. She respects the history and practice of natural medicine, including that of the Native American culture, a people who pass wisdom to the next generation through storytelling.

Listen to the visualizations she has included on the CD and take note of what messages your body and your mind might be sending you. Give yourself the time to do this healing work. Through similar visualizations I have come to appreciate the unique way our bodies and our minds have the ability to support and nurture the other.

Now when I lose my footing and take a tumble, literally or figuratively, I have a resource to help me get back on my feet.

Marie Osmond
July 3, 2001

HOW TO USE THIS BOOK

This book is intended to be used in combination with the compact discs attached inside the book. At the end of each chapter, you will be directed to make yourself comfortable and listen to a specific track on one of the CDs. These are creative visualizations that will guide you in discovering more about your own subconscious beliefs, thoughts and emotions that may be allowing your body to express illness.

Creative visualizations use the power of imagination to affect change. We are using this creative power constantly, though we may not be aware of it, and often in negative ways. What mother has not imagined something terrible happening to a child or a spouse when they are not home at the expected time? When our bodies experience a painful symptom, how often do we imagine something to be terribly wrong? The processes on these CDs allow us to use this imaginative power to create positive thoughts and emotions, which automatically creates positive reactions in our bodies.

When you are ready to listen to the CD, I urge you to find a quiet place, without noises that will distract you. Do these exercises alone or with a friend, relative, or therapist with whom you feel completely comfortable sharing the deepest parts of yourself. Each visualization lasts 25 to 30 minutes. Make sure that you will not be interrupted; for example, do this exercise at a time when your children are at school or in bed, and take the phone off the hook. Find a relaxing position to sit or lay in. However, if you fall asleep when you are laying down, I encourage you to sit. If at anytime you feel like you can't deal with the issues arising for you during the exercise, stop and turn off the CD. You may desire to discuss these issues with a therapist and work through them before you complete the exercise at another time.

Those who suffer from Post-Traumatic Stress Disorder or Dissociative Disorder who desire to use these CDs should make sure that someone with whom you feel safe is with you during these exercises, especially during Dream Picture 4, so that if you experience an abreaction (a memory that feels like you are actually experiencing it) they can assist you through it. Ask your therapist if this is something that would work for you.

There are various religious beliefs expressed in the book and in the creative visualizations. These are not in the book to persuade you to believe in them or join any specific church, but simply as a tool to allow you to discover the universal truths that are inside you. You may find that you do not agree with everything that is said. That is not important. What is important is that you find thoughts, emotions and beliefs that lift you and allow you to find peace rather than drag you down and allow you to feel guilty and depressed. Use this book as a tool to find the healing place in your heart and you will be lifted and comforted.

(Read Prologue before proceeding to Chapter 1)

Judith S. Moore, D.O.

PROLOGUE

He couldn't find the phone. It was ringing and ringing, but no matter where he looked, he couldn't find it. The frustration built and the ringing continued, until finally it awakened George from his dream. He reached over to the nightstand and clumsily grabbed at the phone in the dark. The receiver fell on the floor. George swept his hand across the floor searching for it until his wife, June, finally sat up in bed and switched on the bedside lamp. "I know you resist modern technology, but a little electricity might help here." Blinking in the 75-watt light, George found the receiver. "'Lo," he answered.

George was a man of few words. He was kind and generous and hardworking, but he didn't talk much. A few "yeps" and an "okay," and he hung up the phone. Pulling his tall, lanky frame out of bed, he gathered up yesterday's overalls from a hook on the back of the door and put them on. He turned, nodded at June, and mumbled, "Back in awhile."

"What? Where on earth are you going at this hour?" June asked, concern in her voice. George knew she was worried because he liked his sleep and didn't let much drag him away from it.

"Some folks got themselves stuck in the snow out on the freeway," he told his wife. "That was the sheriff's office. They can't get to them because the plows ain't been there yet, and it'll be hours 'fore they can. Because our farm is closest to them, the sheriff thought I could get to them with my tractor."

June sat up. "Oh, those poor folks! Why on earth are they driving in the middle of the night in the worst storm of the decade? You go get them, George. I'll open the heat vents in George Jr.'s bedroom. They can stay there. I'll get extra blankets and hot chocolate and…" She pulled her housecoat over her nightgown and pattered off telling herself all she needed to do. George looked

1

after her as he put on his boots. He was always amazed at how much June loved a good crisis. He chuckled as he left the house.

"Thank heavens the tractor cabin is heated," George thought as he slowly traveled the back roads. He was grateful that he didn't have to travel through this driving snow and biting cold in his old open tractor. June was insistent that they get this tractor with the air-conditioned and heated cabin. She pampered him because he was nearing fifty-five, and he had resisted because he didn't want to feel old. But right now he was mighty glad he had the heated cabin, especially for the snow-bound folks he was headed to pick up. He laughed, imagining having to coax them from the shelter of their car to ride in the pelting snow on an open-air tractor. They would have thought he was crazy. "Yep, I'm sure glad June got her way."

The nearest freeway entrance was a good forty-five minutes away, and George didn't want those poor folks to wait that long in this cold, so he entered the freeway through an area near a bridge that wasn't fenced. The freeway was empty except for the deepening blanket of snow. The sheriff had said they closed the freeway about a half-hour before he called.

The windshield wiper was barely keeping up with the heavy, inch-sized flakes as the large tires of the tractor moved slowly but steadily through two-foot drifts. George peered in the headlight beam, but could barely see ten feet ahead. After half an hour on the freeway, even as slow as he was going, he almost missed the hazard lights of the Camry in the gully to the side of the freeway, covered with snow. "Boy, have they got themselves into trouble. I don't think my tractor can get that car out of there." He pulled his hat down over his ears, wrapped the ends of his neck-scarf inside his coat and lifted his collar against the wind as he climbed out of the tractor. He worried that he might be too late. He climbed down the gully and tapped on the snowy window of the stranded car.

June began pacing. George had been gone for over two hours. She had a strong faith that God watched over her husband, especially when he was out doing good, but she couldn't help getting a little nervous as she watched the storm raging on. It was after five a.m. Soon the cows would need to be milked. That thought calmed her.

"George has never missed a milking. He'll be here soon." And sure enough, she heard the roar of the tractor engine outside the kitchen door. She raced to the door as George helped a woman out of the tractor. Then a man jumped out of the cab.

"June, I think these folks could use some of your emergency hot chocolate. I'll put the tractor away." George led them into the kitchen and June took over.

"Oh, you poor souls! We'll get you fixed up in no time. My name is June Woodbury. Let me take your coats and you can wrap up in these blankets. Sit here at the kitchen table. That's right. Here, let me help you take your shoes off and we'll wrap blankets around your feet, too. We'll get you warm in no time."

"Thank you so much!" the man said. "I'm John Carter. This is my wife, Anne."

"We're pleased to have you here, certainly. I'm so glad George was able to find you!" June poured some hot chocolate and set warmed-up homemade bread on a dish in front of them. John gratefully started sipping the hot chocolate and eating the bread with relish, but Anne just sat there, staring at the food.

June took a good look at the couple. They were younger, probably in their early thirties. Their clothes were well made and expensive. The man was dark-haired, and haggard lines detracted from the handsome features of his face. His dark eyes looked haunted as he carefully watched his wife. The woman was pretty, but thin and pale. That was the best description for her. Her hair was thin and pale, her face was thin and pale, her dress was thin and pale. "She looks like one of those anorexic girls on the front of a fashion magazine," June thought.

June placed a motherly hand on Anne's arm. "Honey, if you don't like the food, we can fix something else. I'm sorry we don't have coffee for you, but we're Mormons and don't drink coffee. Is that what you're wanting?"

The pale woman looked up at June, and tears started spilling over. "I'm sorry," she whispered, putting her trembling hand to her mouth.

John jumped up and put his arms around her thin shoulders. "Anne's been sick for awhile. I'm sure being stuck in the freezing cold for hours was more than she could take. It isn't your food. She can't seem to tolerate dairy, wheat, and anything with sugar.

I think the best thing for her right now is to let her rest. Do you have an extra couch or anything that she could lay on?"

"Oh, you poor souls!" June repeated. "You're lucky that our oldest son is on his mission. We have an extra bedroom, all heated up, with extra blankets on the bed. Let me show you where to go, and then I'll bring in some herbal tea to help her insides warm up."

George woke their son Tyler and they went out to milk the cows and feed the animals. After settling her visitors, June asked her eldest daughter, Michelle, to help her put together a "proper breakfast" for the family. June fretted over what to feed her new guest. If she couldn't eat dairy or wheat, what else couldn't she eat, and what was in the pantry to feed her? June loved to cook and to feed and fuss over people, but she hadn't come up against this situation before. Her mind was so absorbed with this dilemma that she jumped when her visitor cleared his throat behind her.

"I didn't mean to startle you." John was standing in the kitchen doorway, the light from the hallway silhouetting the defeated shoulders on his well-built body. "We certainly appreciate your husband's rescue and your kindness for inviting us into your home. No, don't stop your work. I'm sure we're an intrusion on your busy schedule."

June straightened her apron over her matronly figure and said kindly, "Here, sit down. You must be so tired. Please tell me why you were out in this awful storm in the middle of the night. I'm sure there must be an important reason."

John nervously cleared his throat again, and, leaning on the doorframe, started telling their story. "We're from a suburb near Detroit. I'm an auto engineer. We've got three kids, ages five to ten. Anne, my wife, has been ill with one thing or another since our five-year-old was born."

June motioned again for John to sit down, and he gratefully accepted. "The doctors didn't know what was wrong with her for a long time," John explained. "She has no energy and says she aches all the time. She can't seem to fight off germs and catches anything that's going around. She's had bronchitis a bunch of times and pneumonia twice. She was always on antibiotics, but now she's starting to react to them and is afraid to take them."

"My goodness," exclaimed June. "That sounds like a hard way to live."

John nodded and sighed. "The last doctor Anne went to diagnosed her with chronic fatigue syndrome and fibromyalgia, but no one seems to know what to do so that she can get better. They give her medicines to reduce her symptoms, but she reacts to them and gets sicker. Now she also can't tolerate most foods or anything with a strong scent. She can only eat a few things. She has been getting thinner and weaker. What's worse, though, is she's constantly depressed. I can't remember the last time she laughed."

John leaned his forehead in his hands and spoke in a low voice. "I worry that she is going to die of malnutrition." He looked back up at June with his haunted look. "I don't understand it, and I'm afraid that sometimes my fear comes out as anger. I worry about the kids, too. They don't really know their mother as a healthy or happy person."

June shook her head. "That's a terrible thing you folks are going through. But with your wife so sick, what are you doing in the mountains of Utah in the middle of the worst snow storm we've had in years?"

John sighed again and leaned back in his chair. "We heard of a clinic in Utah that treats these types of problems. Our appointment is today. But the snowstorm slowed us down, and we ended up having to drive all night to make it in time. The storm kept getting worse all the way through Wyoming. Anne thought we should stop in Evanston. I should have listened to her. We couldn't go faster than 15-20 miles an hour, and you know the rest of the story. I called for help on our cell phone, and lucky for us your husband saw us in the ditch."

"Well, you had a real miracle!" June exclaimed. "Cell phones often don't work in these mountains, especially in a storm such as this. You must have angels watching over you."

"I think our angels have given up," John sighed. "Many people have been praying for Anne, but as much as we pray for her to get better, she's still on a downward slope." John looked down at his hands on the table and frowned, accentuating the haggard lines of his face. "My kids need their mother and she can't take care them. I've used up all my vacation time at work to take her to doctors.

I'm in danger of losing my job if I take any more time off. Our credit cards are at the limit because our insurance doesn't cover all the costs. Anne is a saint. I don't understand how a merciful God can let her suffer, and the kids, too. We're not sure anymore if God hears us and cares about us."

"Well, I'm sorry to hear that," June sighed, "because if Anne loses her faith, what is there to get better for?"

John lifted his head and looked again at June. "I'm sorry. I know I'm complaining. I'm sure you don't need the burden of all our problems."

June smiled. "Never mind that. It's good to get the weight off your shoulders once in a while. But right now our first concern is how to get you out of here and to your doctor. We've already had three feet of snow, and I just heard on the radio that the storm is not expected to let up for two more days. We are fifteen miles from the nearest town. Even the kids' school has been cancelled. The freeways are closed. Your car is so far out of the way and so far down the ditch, George doesn't know how long it will take to get it out. I just don't see any way that you can make that appointment today, or for several days, for that matter."

June placed a plate of eggs and potatoes in front of John, and poured him a tall glass of milk. "Fresh from the cow last night. It's so cold out, the poor Bossie cows were refrigerating their own milk!" June laughed with a mock shiver. "You've never tasted milk like this. Go ahead and eat, and then get a little rest. You're welcome to call your kids from here to let them know where you are. Let me get our two youngest up and going on their chores, and when George returns we'll discuss our options."

The family had completed breakfast and their chores. George lit a fire in the living room, and the children pulled out the Monopoly game. June was still in the kitchen preparing a vegetable-beef soup for lunch when John emerged from the bedroom. He looked careworn and worried as he sat down at the kitchen table. June served him up some home-canned peaches, and George soon joined them. As George sat at the table he chuckled. "You're making June very happy today. She's happiest when she's got a houseful of full stomachs."

John smiled at George, but the smile quickly turned to a look of concern. "My wife seems to be getting a fever and a terrible cough. I'm afraid she's heading into bronchitis again. I should probably get her to a doctor, but I don't know what a doctor could do."

June and George looked at each other, and George nodded. "The nearest doctor is thirty miles away in Coalsville," said June. "We could try and get you there in the tractor, but it would be a long trip for a sick woman in this storm. George and I think we have a better idea. We are going to take you and Anne to Grandmother's house."

John looked confused. "What would your grandmother do for Anne?"

"Oh, she's not our grandmother," explained June. "That's just what folks have always called her. Grandmother learned folk medicine as a child from her grandmother, and then she went to school to become a registered nurse. She worked in the hospital for a few years, but when she began having children, she stayed home and used her knowledge on her own children. Sometimes situations would come up like now when people couldn't get to a doctor, and they went to Grandmother for help. Grandmother always made a difference for them. She only sees sick people in emergencies like this, but mostly she helps folks around here stay healthy. Even more important, Grandmother is a wise, wise woman who knows how to heal hearts."

"But I'm not sure anything is wrong with Anne's heart," said John. "All the tests have shown that her heart seems healthy, even though she gets palpitations. Besides, I'm not sure about doing "weird" stuff with Anne. Lots of people back home had all these ideas of things Anne should be taking. She was so desperate that she tried them all, against my wishes. She spent a lot of money, and nothing really helped over the long run. What can this woman's folk medicine do that all the modern doctors can't?"

"It's not the body's heart that Grandmother heals. It's the heart of the soul," June stated quietly.

"Well, how is that going to help Anne's cough? How can healing the heart of her soul make her better?" John asked.

George shyly broke into the conversation. "That we don't know. We just know that it does. But your wife is too sick to make another long journey in the tractor. Grandmother is on the next farm over. Let us take you to her. If anyone can assist your wife, she can."

"I'll have to trust you on this one," John relented. "Anne definitely needs help. Thank you for understanding."

They all looked up when they heard a groan in the kitchen doorway. Anne was holding onto the doorframe. Her voice was so weak they scarcely heard her. "I don't feel so well, John." She lost her hold and fainted, slumping to the floor.

Chapter 1

WHO AM I?

I'm dead," Anne thought, as she opened her heavy eyelids and saw a woman with a halo standing near her. As the woman turned around, Anne saw that the halo was actually pure white hair pulled up into a loose bun on top of a gentle, wrinkled face. Anne tried to sit up but felt something warm and heavy on her chest. She wanted to ask where she was and where John was, but found herself coughing instead. Searing pain ripped through her chest with every cough.

"Oh, you're awake! No, don't get up, honey, you're lungs are working too hard just getting air. Don't you worry, I've got you all fixed up. Here, take this syrup for your cough." Anne took the spoonful and relaxed. The woman's voice was sweet and soothing, and something about her made Anne know that everything was all right.

"I'm Grandmother, dear. My real name is Hannah Taylor, but everyone calls me Grandmother. George and June brought you here. This is the best place for you to be right now. Your husband talked George into taking him to Coalsville to see if they could get a doctor to come out. He's very worried about you. June had to go back to her kids. It's just you and me, sweetheart, so we have a chance to get to know each other."

Anne looked around the room. It was a simple room with colorful tie rugs placed on a shining wooden floor. The bed was of pine, with the baseboard and posters carved in a simple design and polished smooth. Several pillows at her back propped her up so she could breathe easier. A patchwork quilt covered her. Steam was rising from a humidifier on the floor at the base of her bed. A rocking chair was in the corner next to the bed, with a nightstand between the bed and the chair. A porcelain lamp and a Bible were on the nightstand. The window was covered with white Quaker-lace curtains. There was a wide chest by the wall with bowls, bottles, and bags of leaves on it. Grandmother was working by the chest. She approached Anne with a teacup in her hand.

"Here, honey, drink this up. We've got a nice tea to calm that cough and get the mucus out of your lungs. It has some comfrey root, mullein, valerian root, skullcap, tincture of lobelia and a dash of cayenne."

Anne didn't know what Grandmother was talking about, but she took the offered cup and started sipping. It was bitter and the pepper was burning to her tongue; nevertheless she felt warmth going into her chest, easing the tightness. She continued to sip slowly. She put her hand to the heaviness on her chest and discovered a wet, warm cloth.

"It's a poultice, dear. You've got a paste of herbs on your chest to draw out the infection, with a hot, wet towel over it. I've got mustard, rosemary, more lobelia and mullein, with a couple of chopped cloves of garlic, mixed in olive oil and spread over your chest. The poultice is my workhorse."

As Anne finished the tea, she started coughing again. She struggled to sit up because she felt she was choking. The pain was still there, but not as severe, and she coughed up a lot of mucus, some of it with a tinge of blood.

"That's what we want," Grandmother said patting Anne on the back. "We don't want to stop the cough; just make it easier. It's important to get the mucus out."

Grandmother then pulled out a small bottle with little round, white pellets. "I put some of these in your cheek before while you were sleeping. It's time for another dose. Just put the little balls under your tongue." Anne lifted her tongue between coughs as Grandmother gave her the dose. The pellets were sweet tasting. "This is a homeopathic remedy, dear. I gave you Aconitum when you first arrived to ward off the effects of the cold, but now I'm giving you Phosphorus, which will stop any bleeding in your lungs and allow them to begin healing." Again, Anne didn't know what she was talking about, but the cough began to ease and she was able to lean back and rest.

Anne didn't know how long she had slept, but she felt a little stronger. She opened her eyes to see Grandmother, rocking in the antique rocking chair next to the bed with her head back and her eyes closed. She could tell it was still daylight, though the storm hid the sun. She heard a clock ticking, and looked above her head to see a large, intricately carved cuckoo clock. She sat up to see the time and started coughing again.

"It's only 11:30, dear." Grandmother sat forward in the rocking chair. "You slept deeply but not very long. Still, your rest was much more quiet this time. I don't think your lungs are getting any worse."

"I'm thirsty, Grandmother. Could I have some water?" Grandmother left the room and soon brought a glass of water to Anne. After she took a long, full drink, she leaned back on her pillows. She started coughing again.

"Every time I move, I cough, and then my lungs really hurt. Is there anything to stop the cough?" asked Anne.

"We don't want to stop your cough yet, dear," answered Grandmother. "You need to get the mucus out. That's right, let your cough go deep and bring up that mucus. You should start breathing easier soon.

"I think it's time for a new remedy. Try this. It's called Bryonia." Grandmother gave her some more sugar pellets to put under her tongue. "Bryonia is good for lung problems that are accompanied by thirst for long drinks of water, for coughing that comes with every motion, and for a cough that causes pain." Anne worried a little about taking pills when she didn't know what they were or what they did, but she relaxed as her cough and her pain began to ease a little.

Anne was concerned about John out in the storm. "Is my husband back yet?" she managed to ask before another fit of coughing.

"It'll be a few more hours at least," answered Grandmother. "That tractor doesn't move very fast through this deep snow."

"I wonder if he's called the kids. They don't know where we are. They're staying with John's mother, but we should have called them by now."

"John remembered the children, dear," said Grandmother. "He called them from here before he left to get the doctor. You're welcome to call them whenever you feel the need."

"Thank you, Grandmother. You are being so kind to me." Anne glanced up at the cuckoo clock again.

"Do you like my cuckoo clock?" Grandmother changed the subject to ease Anne's worries. "My Oma's mother brought it from Germany."

"Your who?" Anne asked, almost smiling.

"Oma was what we called my grandmother. It's actually the German word for 'Grandmother.' Oma taught me most everything I know. I have a degree in nursing, but I would be lost without the things Oma taught me. She came to Utah from Germany when she was six years old. Her family was called by the Mormon prophet, Brigham Young, to settle a remote area of Utah. Their first winter there was similar to this one, with deep snow and blinding blizzards, and they ran out of food. There was a tribe of Indians nearby that took compassion on the young family and took them in for the winter."

Grandmother chuckled. "I guess I should call them Native Americans, but I've always called them Indians, and can't remember to be politically correct. My Oma taught me to love and respect the Indians. Anyway, the Indians fed Oma's family and taught them their language. Oma learned to love them and became best friends with one of the girls. Even after that winter she still spent a lot of time with them. She loved their stories and learned about the plants they used for medicine. Oma's mother was a midwife, and had brought herbs and homeopathic remedies from Germany, but there were new herbs here. Oma learned about them from the Indians and then taught her mother how to use them. Oma and her mother became renowned in the area for their gift of healing.

"When I was young, my mother had to work, and Oma would watch me and take me with her when she delivered babies and helped sick folks. Out of all of her children and grandchildren, I was the only one interested in learning what she knew. So she taught me."

"Well, I'm grateful for your Oma, then," said Anne. "This is certainly a nicer place to be than a hospital, and I haven't reacted to any of your medicines."

"Now honey, you know a little about me. I would like to know about you. Who are you?"

"Well, my full name is Anne Elizabeth Carter, and we're from Ann Arbor, Michigan."

"I know that, dear. I want you to tell me who you are."

Anne was a bit confused, but she continued. "Well, John and I have three children, two girls and a boy, ages 10, 8, and 5," said Anne. "My oldest, Tina, is so sweet, really bright, and has been a great help while I've been sick. Then there's Eric, who's a ball of energy. He's been a real handful to deal with, but he's lovable. I think he might be hyperactive. My youngest, Rachel, was diagnosed with autism three years ago. It's taken intense therapy to get her to talk like a two-year-old, which breaks my heart. I love her dearly but she takes every ounce of energy I have."

"I'm glad to know who your children are, dear," said Grandmother quietly. "Now tell me, who are you?"

"What else should I tell you?" questioned Anne. Grandmother didn't answer. Anne was becoming uncomfortable under Grandmother's quiet gaze, searching Anne's face with deep blue eyes, bordered by the lines of many years of smiles.

Anne decided to try again. "Well, I was born in Pennsylvania, the fourth in a family of five children. My father was a coal miner. We lived in company housing. We never had quite enough money, but we never starved. I did pretty well in school and got a scholarship. It was the only way I could go to college. I wanted to be a doctor, and I could have been. However, I met John my senior year, and then I just wanted to be a wife and mother. I don't really regret my decision, but I had no idea how hard being a parent would be. As much as I love my kids, I miss the stimulation of learning and growing outside of my little world. And caring for Rachel has been overwhelming. I often feel like a failure, and sometimes I wonder if I made the right choice. Maybe I should have gone on to medical school. I may have been able to give more to the world."

Grandmother shifted in the rocking chair, continuing her searching gaze. "Now I know about some of your unfulfilled expectations. But Anne, who are you?"

Anne was frustrated. "I don't know what you want. I'm a sick, hurting, depressed, miserable woman who can't properly care for her children and can't keep her husband happy anymore! I'm not sure life is worth living when I'm such a burden to everyone. Is that what you want to know?" Anne started coughing again.

Grandmother gave Anne more of the burning tea, and the coughing subsided. Then Grandmother leaned her head back in the rocking chair and closed her eyes. Anne thought that Grandmother was going to sleep when she heard her say quietly, "Let me tell you a story Oma used to tell me."

*   *   *

No one called him Running Wolf but his mother. The rest of the tribe called him Stick Leg, because when he was born his leg was deformed and looked like a stick. His mother could not have children easily, and while she was carrying him her husband was killed. In their tribe, deformed babies were usually left to die, but Stick Leg's mother had birthed him alone and she kept him, even when she saw his leg. She wrapped him in a colorful blanket and carried him in the cradleboard where no one could see his leg. When he was old enough to scoot out of his blanket, everyone was shocked. However, they were used to having him around, and no one had the heart to kill him. The village elders decided to allow him to live in honor of Shining Crow, his father.

But there were no other children with short, skinny legs and stumps for feet. There was one old man in the village who had lost his leg as a brave warrior, but he was honored. Being born with a stick leg did not bring honor, but shame. Stick Leg could not run fast like the other children. He could not keep up in the hunting games of the other boys. The younger children mimicked his limping gait and the older boys laughed at him. He could never be Running Wolf. He was just Stick Leg.

Stick Leg was happiest when he was alone in the forest watching the animals. In spite of his limp, he had learned to walk quietly. The animals seemed to know that they were safe with him, and did not run away. He felt that he could understand what they were saying, and that they understood him also. He would speak to them with thoughts from his heart. He felt comfortable with the animals in a way that he never felt comfortable with people.

One afternoon Stick Leg was bringing water for his mother from the clear stream that ran through the village. He watched some village boys chase each other with a yearning, wishing that he could join in. Suddenly two boys ran past Stick Leg and bumped into him, throwing him off balance. His lame leg twisted and he fell over, splashing water everywhere. He found himself sitting in a puddle of mud, his leg throbbing from the fall. His eight-year-old heart tried to be strong, but the tears slipped down his cheeks. The boys laughed and ran on.

"The least they could do is help you up!" exclaimed Singing Bird, running up to him. Singing Bird was his eleven-year-old cousin. She had taken care of him when he was younger, but her help embarrassed him now.

"I can get up by myself. I do not need help." Stick Leg struggled to his feet.

"You are right, Stick Leg," Singing Bird said. "You do not need help anymore. But come and let mother look at your leg. You walk like it hurts."

Singing Bird's mother, White Feather, was a medicine woman. She was not like Standing Bear, the Medicine Man, who was in charge of all the ceremonies. She took care of the sick people, especially the women, children and old ones. Everyone loved White Feather. Stick Leg was in pain from the fall, so he hobbled slowly behind his cousin to White Feather's lodge.

White Feather examined the leg. "It is not serious," she told him. "There is not even any swelling." She rubbed the leg to bring blood to the soreness and gave Stick Leg some weak willow bark tea. "Your pain will be gone by the time you finish this tea," she said soothingly.

Stick Leg sipped the tea, and slowly the pain went away. He smiled at White Feather, saying, "Thank you, White Feather, for using your magic on me."

"This is not magic, Stick Leg," said White Feather, "just Mother Earth giving us her gifts. I'm glad you came to see me today. I have been wanting to talk to you, or rather, to have you talk to me." White Feather sat down across from Stick Leg. "Stick Leg, tell me, who are you?"

Stick Leg thought this was a strange question, as White Feather had known him all his life, but he knew that he must show respect and answer all of her questions. "I am Stick Leg, son of Shining Crow, your brother, who died in battle just before I was born, and

Dancing Water, who kept me alive when I should be dead."

White Feather looked at him kindly and said again, "Who are you?"

Stick Leg thought for a moment, and then answered, "I am named Running Wolf, but I am not Running Wolf, because I cannot run, and I am not strong and cunning and a great hunter as is the wolf."

"Then who are you?" said White Feather.

Stick Leg wanted to please White Feather. He tried again. He must be honest. "I am a boy with a leg like a stick. My leg is weak, and I walk with a limp and move too slowly. I am a burden on my mother because I cannot do the work of a man, or even the work of a boy. I am worthy only of being laughed at. I am not worthy of our people. No one else is like me."

White Feather sighed. "It is true that no one else is like you, Stick Leg, but what you have just told me is not who you are."

"That is not who I am?" queried Stick Leg, surprised. "Then who am I?"

"This question is not for me to answer," said White Feather softly. "You must answer this question for yourself. Do not look so puzzled. The answer is inside you. Go to the animals. You will find the answer as you watch them."

That night Stick Leg thought about White Feather's question. "Who am I?" he thought. "If I am not the boy with the bad leg who should never have lived, who is despised among his own people, then who am I? Tomorrow I will get up early and go into the forest so that I may find the answer."

Stick Leg crept into his Watching Place, an opening under a willow bush where deer used to sleep. The bush was at the edge of a beautiful little clearing, the birthplace of a sparkling, gurgling spring. Many birds and animals came to the clearing to drink from the clear pool or eat the tender shoots at the brook's edge.

The darkness just before dawn found Stick Leg sitting very still in his place at the edge of the bush, the green leaves of the willow branches rustling in the gentle breeze behind him. His sharp ears listened for other sounds above the babbling of the spring. The night had been warm, and he knew that the deer would soon be getting a last drink before they went to bed. There were five deer that regularly came to the clearing—two does and three fawns. There had been one other doe, but she was no longer with them. Stick Leg suspected that she had been part of their tribal feast last month, after the hunters had returned. The orphaned fawn had become very timid and fearful, coming into the clearing only after the others had arrived, jumping at every sound.

As the dark sky began to lighten from black to gray, shadows emerged from the forest, which became the deer. Two fawns bounded into the clearing and froze on seeing Stick Leg. The does entered slowly, eating, lifting their heads abruptly when they saw the young boy. They stared at him for a moment, then, sensing no danger, continued eating. Only then did the fawns move again, going to the pool to drink. Stick Leg sat very still, watching the eyes of the third fawn as it remained fearful in the scrub at the edge of the clearing.

"It is all right, little fawn," Stick Leg thought with all the energy of his boy heart. "I will not hurt you. I will not move and frighten you. I will let you eat and drink in peace."

The fawn entered the clearing slowly. "I am afraid of your smell. A smell similar to yours was present when the sharp stick with feathers entered my mother. She fell, and the animals with two legs like you took her away. Now I am alone. The others let me come with them, but I do not belong to them. I do not want a stick with feathers in my side. I am afraid of your smell."

Stick Leg remained still. "Look at the other deer, little fawn. They are not afraid. They know I will not hurt them. You have been here with me before. I have never hurt you or frightened you."

The spotted fawn stood still, looking at Stick Leg. "That was before my mother was gone. Now I know that I can be hurt, that I can die. Now I know what it is like to be alone, to have others treat me differently. Now I am always afraid of being hurt. I am afraid of how other animals and other deer will treat me. I can't take a chance that you will hurt me." The fawn suddenly turned and bounded back into the protection of the forest, blending in with the brush.

Stick Leg pondered the plight of this little fawn for a moment. He felt a kinship with this frightened animal. "I know what it is! Little Fawn Who Lives in Fear, you are teaching me just as White Feather said! When I was very little, I did not know that I was different. I was happy with Mother. Then Crooked Feather told me that my mother should have killed me when I was born because my leg was deformed. Others laughed at me. I started living in fear. I was afraid that I was not good enough because of how the others treated me. I judged myself and reacted to what others said and did. I see now that I am not what others say about me, or the result of how they treat me. I am still the same boy that was happy before I knew all of these things."

A strong feeling of love flooded warmly through the body of Stick Leg. He knew the truth of what he was saying to the fawn. He knew that he was the same boy as that happy little child, and that his experiences since then did not lessen his worth. "Little Fawn, take courage. You are the same fawn that you were before your mother was taken. Your knowledge that others can hurt you does not change who you are. It just changes what you know. You trusted me before; please trust me again. Be cautious, but not fearful. Trust that the Great Spirit will warn you of danger if it is not time for you to die. Trust that if it is time, all will be well for you."

The fawn again stepped slowly into the clearing and hesitantly dipped its nose into the brook for a drink. "You do not feel as scary as you did before. But it is very hard. It is hard when I am all alone and the others don't play with me."

Stick Leg smiled. "I know, Little Fawn. I know how you feel. I felt worthless because no one played with me. But now I see that this has nothing to do with who I am. If the children don't want to be with me, that is their problem, not mine. My problem is to learn to love them even as they judge me. They are judging me by how I look and by what I can and cannot do, but their judgment is not truth. How others treat me may affect me for good or ill, but it has nothing to do with who I really am."

The fawn looked up as a pheasant swept into the clearing and posed on a rock next to the spring. His colors radiated brilliantly as the sun peeked over the horizon, shining directly on him. He began preening.

Stick Leg was pleased to see him. "Good morning, Mr. Pheasant," Stick Leg said with his heart. "Your colors are exceptionally beautiful today."

"I know. I am the most brightly colored pheasant in the forest. All the hens are attracted to me. I am well-respected because of my beautiful colors and long feathers."

Stick Leg chuckled. "I know someone like you, Mr. Pheasant. His name is Spotted Owl. He spends a lot of time rubbing oil on his muscles and painting his face and braiding his very long hair, adorning each braid with brightly colored feathers. He tells every-one to look at how great he is. The women admire him because he looks like a great warrior. My mother says looking like a great war-rior does not make him a great warrior."

Stick Leg frowned. "Spotted Owl told the council that they should get rid of me because my leg is ugly and useless, that only perfect people should belong to this tribe. I cried when I heard what he said. I thought because I did not look perfect, I could not be perfect. My mother keeps saying that how the body looks has nothing to do with who you are. Now as I watch you preen, I think she may be right!"

"Humph!" said the pheasant, as he slowly drew a long, irides-cent feather through his beak. Then with a disdainful look at Stick Leg, he lifted himself proudly into the air and flew away.

The deer finished their drinking and were leaving the clearing, stopping frequently to nibble on the tender clover. The little fawn turned for one last look at Stick Leg. "I remember how happy and trusting I was before mother left. I want to be that way again. I will work on letting go of my fear and trusting the Great Spirit."

Stick Leg sat alone, considering what he had learned so far. He heard a rustle in the leaves above him and looked up. A squirrel was busy gathering acorns and seeds from the trees overhead.

"Stop and come talk to me, Brown Squirrel. I want to learn from you, too."

The squirrel stopped for a moment, then hurried across the branch and hopped onto the next tree. "I cannot stop. I must keep gathering. I must be ready for the winter."

"Brown Squirrel, I saw your hole last week, and you have plen-ty of food to last the winter already," Stick Leg urged.

"I cannot stop. I must have the most. What if someone steals my food? Or what if my lazy neighbors run out of nuts before the win-ter is over? Then I will feel obligated to give some to them. Everyone knows that I always have the most food for the winter. I cannot stop working."

"Oh my, Brown Squirrel," thought Stick Leg, "I know someone like you, too. He is in my tribe. Crazy Hawk thinks he is great because he owns more sheep and goats than anyone else in the tribe. But it is not enough. He keeps working to find ways to get more. He will only use the best deer hides for his clothes. His wives have beautiful jewelry of silver, and their clothes are adorned with dyed porcupine quills. I can tell by the way he looks at my mother that he thinks she is not important because she does not own very many things. Sometimes I feel ashamed when Crazy Hawk is around, because our clothes are not of fine deerskin, and we only own two goats and one sheep. However, Crazy Hawk never shares his meat with us to honor the spirit of the great warrior, Shining Crow, as other families do."

Brown Squirrel ignored him and dashed here and there, flicking his tail and searching for nuts.

"Brown Squirrel," exclaimed Stick Leg, "I am learning from you, even though you will not stop to talk to me. You believe that who you are depends on what you own. I have believed that, too. I thought that I was not worth anything because I did not have nice clothes or possessions. That is a lie. What I possess has nothing to do with who I really am. All I own really belongs to Mother Earth, and she can claim it at any time. It does not change who I am! Good-by, Brown Squirrel. Thank you for being my teacher!"

Stick Leg continued to sit completely still. The soft wind cooled his face as the sun grew higher in the sky. The grass and wildflowers bent to the song of the breeze. A honeybee wended its way among the dancing flowers.

"Honey Bee, do you have time for me? The animals are teaching me today."

The bee flew to a patch of clover near Stick Leg. "I am busy; there is much work for me to do. I am gathering pollen, Stick Leg, and then I must take it to the hive and help with the work there. If I do not gather enough pollen, all the other bees will think I have been shirking my duty."

"But might your duty also include teaching me?" queried Stick Leg.

"I am sorry, but I am too bizzzy," answered the honeybee, moving on to the next patch of flowers.

Stick Leg watched the little bee moving quickly from flower to flower. "You are busy, Honey Bee, and I always see you working hard. But I do not think you are busy like Brown Squirrel, so you can own a lot of things. Do you work that hard just so the others will not think that you are lazy? Possibly. I also believe that you work hard because you believe that is what you are supposed to do; working hard is the only thing that gives your life meaning and worth."

"I am bizzzy. I must go now." The honeybee carried its load of nectar back into the forest.

Stick Leg considered what lesson he was to learn from Honey Bee. He knew that hard work was important. Did he have less worth than others in the tribe if he couldn't work as long or as hard as they could? Was his life less meaningful? Some of the tribe members thought this was true.

Stick Leg remembered his grandmother. She worked hard all her life. When he wanted to talk to her or show her something, she was always too busy. When she became sick, she worried about the things she couldn't do. "I'm worthless, just sitting here like an old cracked water pot," she would complain, and then she would try to work anyway, even though she was sick.

When Grandmother died last year, Mother held her limp body close and cried that Grandmother had worked herself to death. Later Mother told Stick Leg that the Great Spirit does not require any of us to run faster than we are able. She told Stick Leg that, if he trusted in the Great Spirit, the Great Spirit would help Stick Leg win the race anyway. Stick Leg did not understand. His leg would never be fast enough to win the races of the children. He now knew that Mother was talking about the Race of Life.

"I know what the lesson is from Honey Bee!" thought Stick Leg. "My grandmother thought that what she accomplished was what gave her worth, but my mother taught me that our work does not make us who we are. Hard work is important for our growth and our learning, but it does not create who we are. Many, like me, are weak in their bodies. Others have weaknesses in their minds or in their thoughts that keep them from accomplishing many things. The Great Spirit does not require me to do what everyone else does. If I do the best I can, that is enough. My worth is not dependent on my accomplishments. My accomplishments are not who I really am!"

"What about the accomplishments of your family? Are you more valuable because your father was a great warrior?" Stick Leg jumped at the new sound. He had not been watching carefully. A wolf was entering the clearing. "Do not be afraid, Stick Leg, I have already eaten and will not harm you. But be more cautious. If my family was hungry, you would be easy prey." The wolf's mate and cubs now entered the clearing.

"I will be more cautious, Grey Wolf. I have been learning from the animals today and my thoughts wandered. I will be more observant even as I am thinking."

The wolf trotted over to the brook. "That is good, Stick Leg. That is what I have taught my children. Look at my cubs. Most of them are learning well and make Mother and me proud in front of the Pack. But little White Socks over there has not been learning well. Look at him running around and barking. How can he be a good hunter with all that jumping and noise? He cannot catch a mouse, so he tries to steal his brother's mouse. Mother and I feel like failures. If we were better parents, he would be able to learn what is important and would act like a good wolf cub. As leader of the Wolf Pack, the others watch me as an example. What kind of example am I when I cannot control my own cub? White Socks makes us ashamed in front of our pack."

Stick Leg considered what the wolf had said. "I, too, know children that make their parents ashamed. Crooked Feather, one of the boys a little older than me, does not always follow the ways of our people. Sometimes he is mean to animals. He is often rude and does not show respect for his elders. He does not like to work, and he always complains. I have heard his parents say that he lowers the worth of their good names."

"That's just what I've felt," exclaimed the wolf.

"But if what we accomplish is not who we really are," questioned Stick Leg, "then how could the actions of our family create who we are? We cannot always control how our family acts. My mother could not make my grandmother work less. She could not keep my father from going into battle and dying. She cannot make me work harder than I am able to. Just because my aunt is a medicine woman, who is loved by all, that does not make me a better person. You teach White Socks the best you know how, but he cannot stay still. If you are not able to control how he acts, how can that lower your worth? I believe that the good and the bad actions of our families do not make us who we are. It may affect our lives, but it is not who we are."

Grey Wolf stood up to leave. "You are right. Mother and I are not bad parents just because White Socks has a difficult time controlling himself. I will show White Socks how much I love him, and I will not be so harsh with him. He will learn to be a better hunter when he goes hungry. Thank you, Stick Leg." The wolf family moved back into the forest.

The sun was high overhead. He must go. Stick Leg knew his mother would be waiting for him to fetch the water to fill the cooking pot for the noon meal. As he quietly limped back through the forest, he saw the great eagle soar to the top of the tallest tree and settle in his nest of sticks.

"Great Eagle," Stick Leg's earnest boy-heart called, "I wish to learn from you. You see the world from the top of the skies. You have great knowledge and wisdom. I wish to have knowledge such as yours so that I may be a wiser person."

"Man child," stated the great eagle, "knowledge does not make you wise, nor does it make you great."

The large eagle hopped onto a lower branch, and cocked his head towards Stick Leg. "When man's head is full of facts, he often confuses facts for wisdom. When a man thinks he knows everything, he learns nothing, for he closes his ears and his heart. The knowledge that is most worthwhile may never be learned. Knowledge can be used for good or for evil. You can be wise without having great knowledge. You can have great knowledge and still be a fool. Listen to your heart, man child. There is already great wisdom there. Knowing many things may help you in life, but knowledge has nothing to do with who you really are."

The eagle spread his wings and started flying in wide circles overhead. "Consider who you are, man child. Consider the knowledge that is deep within you. What is the wisdom within that knows how to turn a meal of goat cheese and corn into muscles and hair, that causes you to grow from a baby into a man? How does the man baby know how to suck milk from his mother, or to cry when he is in need? How does the foal know how to stand up and walk? How do my young ones know how to fly? Within you is knowledge greater than the greatest chieftain, or the wisest medicine man, or the largest eagle. Where does this knowledge come from? Consider who you are."

"Thank you, Great Eagle. You have taught me well. I will gain knowledge to do good, but that knowledge does not make me who I am. And I am truly striving to learn who I am." Stick Leg traveled on, pondering what the great eagle had said.

As Stick Leg came into the village, he took the earthen pot by his mother's door and headed to the stream. As he was coming around the corner of a lodge, he heard a dog yelping. "Get away from here, you ugly, good-for-nothing dog," he heard Crooked Feather yell. "You are not good enough to be at my door. If you come here again I will kill you and eat you!" The dog fled with his tail between his legs. Stick Leg did not want to meet the anger of Crooked Feather, so he waited on the side of the lodge until he heard the boy go back inside. Then he headed toward the stream, where he found the dog whining and licking his leg.

Stick Leg knelt and stroked the dog's thick fur. "Dog, why are you whining? What happened to you?"

The dog licked Stick Leg's hand. "I am nothing but an ugly, no-good dog. I was eating a scrap that had fallen by Crooked Feather's lodge, and he kicked me. Nobody wants me. Nobody likes me. You are the only one that is nice to me."

Stick Leg shook his head. "Dog, just because Crooked Feather said you were no good does not mean that you are no good. You keep the ground clean of scraps. Babies play on top of you and pull your tail. You guard the camp and let us know when danger is near. You do what all good dogs do."

"But Stick Leg, if everyone tells me I'm no good, then that is what I must be," whined the dog.

"Dog, what people say about you has nothing to do with who you are. If one person says good things about you and gives you great honors, you are still the same dog as when the next person kicks you and calls you names. What other people perceive you to be is just their judgment of you. Do not create who you are by what people say or think about you. No one really knows who you are but you and the Great Spirit."

The dog continued to whine, licking his wounds. Stick Leg saw that the dog would not change his mind easily, so he filled the pot and brought it back to his mother. After the noonday meal, he went over to talk to White Feather.

"I have been to see the animals as you told me to, White Feather," Stick Leg reported. "I have learned that who I am is not based on my good or bad experiences, on how my body looks or how strong I am, on how many possessions I have, on what I can accomplish, on how my family acts or what they accomplish, on my knowledge or education, or by what others think of me or perceive me to be. All of these can have an affect on how my life is lived, but they are not who I am."

"These things are all true," responded White Feather, smiling warmly. "You have learned much this morning. These are all the things that you are not, so can you now tell me who you are?"

"I've been thinking about the person who is called 'me' all morning," said Stick Leg slowly. "Each of the animals has their own concerns, problems, beauty, possessions and knowledge, but those are not who they are. I love the animals simply because they are special creations of the Great Spirit. Each one was created for a purpose, and part of their purpose today was to teach me, though most of them did not know this."

Stick Leg shifted and put out his shriveled leg for White Feather to see. "I have been looking at this leg today. I have moved it around, looked at its shape, and felt the thickened skin. I see that this leg is part of me, but it is not 'me.' I could cut it off and I would still be here. I thought of all the parts inside of me, like my stomach and my heart and my brain. I need these parts of me to live on this earth, but they are not 'me.' My flesh is not the real 'me,' and even my brain is not the life-giving intelligence within me. The real 'me' is the spirit within that was created by the Great Spirit. This spirit is Who I Am. Everything else is simply part of my existence on this earth."

Stick Leg paused, and then spoke convincingly. "I am Running Wolf, a creation of the Great Spirit, created for a purpose. My leg, which looks like a stick and keeps me from running with the children, was created for a purpose. I cannot run with the children, but my Spirit can run with the wisdom I gain from being different. I am like Grey Wolf, who loves his family and leads his pack with wisdom. I am special because I am different. I am a teacher because I am different. I am Running Wolf, a spiritual, loving, powerful boy."

Tears were running down White Feather's cheeks. She pulled him close to her as she said, "My son, I see that you have found Love. Loving yourself allows you to build on your talents and strengths rather than dwelling on your weaknesses. Loving yourself allows you to know that your weaknesses *are* your strengths because of how they shape your life and what they teach you."

White Feather knelt down in front of Stick Leg. "You have grown in wisdom beyond your years today. I will approach the Medicine Man. We will have a ceremony so that we may say good-by to Stick Leg and welcome into our tribe the wise Running Wolf."

*　*　*

You're a wonderful storyteller, Grandmother," said Anne softly. "I wish life could be as simple as telling a story. It's hard for me to feel like I measure up in the real world. I've always wanted to feel I have a purpose, or that my life is worthwhile. I don't have any conviction like Stick Leg."

Grandmother went over to the corner and turned on soft music from the small stereo. "Occasionally Oma used to speak to us in a way that created what she called 'Dream Pictures.' Today I believe it is called 'Creative Imagery' or 'Visualizations.' Are you familiar with this?"

Anne shook her head no.

"Well," Grandmother continued, "Oma's Dream Pictures use the imagination to create reality. I hear they are using this process today in cancer centers, where they are having children imagine their white blood cells to be something like Pacman, gobbling up the cancer cells. The imagination can use these symbols to reach the subconscious mind and change the false beliefs that allow a person to get sick. I have changed Oma's Dream Pictures slightly to conform to the modern world, but they are still basically the same as what she taught me. Are you interested in trying one of the Dream Pictures or a creative imagery process to see if you can find out who you are?"

"I don't know, Grandmother," said Anne dubiously. "The subconscious scares me. What if I do something wrong?"

"I don't want you to do anything you feel uncomfortable with, dear," said Grandmother. "This is just a process of allowing yourself to be relaxed and using symbols to bring to mind knowledge that you already have deep inside you. All of the images are merely symbolic, allowing you to reach truths that you already know. You won't get lost in there. In fact, if you feel uncomfortable at any time, you will be able to stop. And it won't change any beliefs or anything about you that you really don't want to change."

"Well, I could try it," answered Anne. "I've tried the tea and the white sugar pills, so I'll trust you on this one, too."

*   *   *

Make yourself comfortable and listen to "Chapter One—Who Am I" on Track 1 of the CD.

Chapter 2

THE LAW OF THE HARVEST

Grandmother, I had no idea that I had so much light!" Anne was leaning back against the gentle embrace of several fluffy pillows, tears streaming down her face.

"I am so glad you could see your dream pictures, dear," said Grandmother. "Now, after experiencing those wonderful things, do you think you could answer my question?" Grandmother paused a moment, and then asked, "Anne Carter, who are you?"

"I know now, Grandmother. I am a woman of light, love and even power!" exclaimed Anne.

"Oh yes, my dear, yes you are. Now you are really beginning to feel your heart, and all of the tender lessons that it has to teach you."

Grandmother glanced at the cuckoo clock. "Well, look, here it is, already past one o'clock. June sent over some delicious broth. If she's not feeding her household, she's feeding the neighborhood! I'll go warm it up. I want you to drink what you can, and then it is time for you to rest. We will let your heart continue to do its healing work on your body while you sleep."

"Cuckoo, cuckoo, cuckoo, cuckoo!" Anne woke up startled, unable to remember where she was. When she tried to sit up, the coughing started. Oh yes, Grandmother's house.

Four o'clock. The storm outside still darkened the bedroom, and twilight would be coming soon. Grandmother was not in the room. She noticed that her chest didn't hurt any more when she coughed, though she was using tissue after tissue. Anne wondered if John had returned.

The door opened and Grandmother entered. "I thought I heard you. You had a good nap. How are you feeling?"

"My chest doesn't hurt anymore, Grandmother, but I feel like I'll never stop coughing. Is John back yet?"

"Not yet, my dear. I expect they'll be back soon. Don't you worry about them. George has lived here all his life and has lots of experience with this kind of weather. John is in good hands." Grandmother pulled down the quilt and bent over Anne to check the poultice. "Oh, my. You've been sweating with fever. Your nightgown is damp. Let's wash off the poultice and give you a bed bath and a change of clothes. You'll feel much better."

Anne was contemplative as Grandmother busied herself getting the washbasin and warm water. As Grandmother was washing her, Anne asked, "Grandmother, if I am as bright and powerful as I saw myself to be, why am I so sick and unhappy?"

"You are thinking good questions, sweet Anne," answered Grandmother as she rinsed out the washcloth in the warm, soapy water. "Have you ever heard of the Law of the Harvest?"

"Isn't that something like you reap what you sow?"

Grandmother nodded as she leaned Anne forward so she could wash her back.

"But Grandmother," Anne protested. "I don't think that applies to me. I really tried to eat a healthy diet and exercise. It didn't keep me from getting sick."

"I wish it were that simple, dear," answered Grandmother. "I believe illness comes because of many reasons, and many of these reasons we will not know of until we cross over to the other side. However, I believe illness often comes because of the Law of the Harvest. Let me tell you another story about Running Wolf."

*   *   *

At the age of ten summers, Running Wolf discovered that he enjoyed the planting season. Accustomed to moving slowly, Running Wolf found that planting corn was a good time to ponder as he made a hole with his stick, dropped the seed in it, spread dirt over the hole with his foot, and took another step to repeat the process over again. The other children were impatient with the slow process, but the repetition suited Running Wolf. He was happy as he planted the corn on this bright, sunny morning.

Crooked Feather sat down heavily on the dirt hill in the next row over and complained, "This is not the work of a warrior. I am almost twelve summers and should not be doing woman's work. Now that the Medicine Man has started teaching you, I do not understand why you volunteered to be here this morning. I do not know why I am the one that had to come plant with you when there are many younger children who could just as easily do the job."

Running Wolf smiled. "They must think you are the best one for the job, Crooked Feather. You can work much faster than the younger children when you choose to."

"No," countered Crooked Feather, "they just wanted to get rid of me. No one wants me around."

"Well, you were cross as a hungry bear this morning," said Running Wolf. "Why were you so upset at your mother?"

"The corn mush tasted a little burned and I would not eat it," said Crooked Feather sourly. "She would not fix me anything else, and I was hungry. I do not know why she does not treat me with the respect that a warrior deserves."

Running Wolf laughed. "If you do not like the results you get, Crooked Feather, change your thoughts and actions so that you may get what you want. Besides, I do not think that you know what hunger really is, as your mother does."

Crooked Feather became defensive. "What do you mean, change myself? I am not to blame if my mother burns the food. And how do you know that my mother knows what hunger is?"

"Crooked Feather," questioned Running Wolf, "would you like to come with me this afternoon to visit the Medicine Man? He told me a story about the tribe that I believe you would find interesting. I know you want to learn the things Standing Bear has been teaching me."

"I do not think that Standing Bear likes me, either," sighed Crooked Feather. "He probably would not let me come with you."

"You expect people to not like you, Crooked Feather, so no matter what they say or do, you take it as a sign that you are right. I know of no one that Standing Bear does not like. If we finish these rows quickly, we will have time to see him after the noonday meal."

Running Wolf smiled as Crooked Feather stood up and started working. "Maybe if I learn some of Standing Bear's secrets," Running Wolf heard him say softly, "the others might respect me more."

He soon caught up with Running Wolf, and they worked silently down the rows together.

"Standing Bear, may we enter and join you for a time?" asked Running Wolf at the entrance to the Medicine Man's lodge.

"Come in, my little friend," answered Standing Bear. "And who else is there hesitating at my door?"

"Crooked Feather is with me today, wise teacher," said Running Wolf as he pulled Crooked Feather into the lodge. "I brought him with me because while we were planting the corn, he had some questions. He does not know why people do not respect him. And he was questioning how his thoughts and actions could have any effect on how people treat him, or on what results he gets. I thought that he deserved to hear the story of what happened to our tribe many years ago."

"Crooked Feather, you are my honored guest," said Standing Bear as he motioned for the boys to sit. "We elders have been amiss. We have not taught our young ones about the last battle with the Others of the Great Valley."

"A battle with the Others of the Great Valley?" Crooked Feather repeated in surprise. "Have they not always been our good friends, bringing us gifts every year?"

"They are our friends now," explained Standing Bear. "But for many generations they were our greatest enemy. We do not know what started the anger. Stories, passed down in our tribe, said that they had stolen our land. The land in the Great Valley has rich soil for good corn, and tall grass for the grazing of sheep and goats. The river and swamps hold many fish. Up here in the mountain valleys the soil is not as rich, and we must work harder for our food. The stories say that we used to live in the Great Valley, but that the Others stole our land."

"That is certainly reason enough to be enemies," said Crooked Feather.

"That is what we always thought, Crooked Feather. But the Others also had stories. They said that one of our chiefs tried to gain power over them in order to make them our slaves, and when his attempt failed, he had the Medicine Man cast a spell on them so that a bad Sickness would come to them every year at the time of the Great Heat. The Sickness killed enough of the Others to keep their tribe from becoming large and great. Each of us had our reasons to hate the other. The result of hating was that we spent much time and many resources in battle and lost many good men."

"If they have stolen our land and we still do not have it back, then we should gather our warriors together and go get it now!" exclaimed Crooked Feather, rising to his feet and puffing out his chest.

The Medicine Man gently nodded to Crooked Feather, directing him to sit down again. "That is exactly what our people thought for many years, and almost every year a new battle was fought," he said. "Then about eleven summers ago, the warriors were having a council, preparing again to go to battle against the Others. Shining Crow, the father of Running Wolf here, said that he had something very important to say. He said that it was so important that he wanted to pass the pipe around before he said it so that everyone would seriously consider what he had to say. You boys were planting corn today, so you may be interested in his words."

"What does planting corn have to do with going into battle?" questioned Crooked Feather.

"Let me answer your question with a question," said Standing Bear. "You have planted many seeds of corn today. What do you expect to grow out of those seeds?"

"Why corn, of course," remarked Crooked Feather.

Standing Bear smiled. "The warriors also thought the question was unusual when Shining Crow asked it. But he explained that we would never get corn from a squash seed, and we would never get squash from the seed of a corn. The corn seed contains all the knowledge and power that is needed to create corn, and the squash seed contains all the knowledge and power that is needed to create squash. This is the Law of the Harvest. Whatever kind of seed you plant, as long as there is sun and rain and good soil to nourish the seed, you will harvest exactly what you planted. It cannot change.

"The warriors were getting restless with all this talk of harvesting, as you are, Crooked Feather, until Shining Crow told them that they had been planting the wrong kind of seeds with the Others. Running Wolf, do you remember what I have told you about the words of your father?"

"Yes, wise teacher," answered Running Wolf. "My father told them that they kept fighting the Others of the Great Valley because they wanted their land back, so that they could harvest more crops. But in all the years of fighting, they had never gotten their land back. He said that they were not getting the crop they wanted so they must be planting the wrong kind of seeds."

"Very good, Running Wolf," said Standing Bear. "Your father understood that because they were sowing seeds of greed, hate and anger, the crops they harvested were the fruits of those feelings: fear of attack, hunger because the warriors were not around to hunt, and widows and orphans. This is what he told the council.

"Shining Crow stood up and lifted the peace pipe in front of him with both hands. 'I am tired of the battles,' he said to the council. 'I am tired of counting coup and claiming that we have won, when the battles are costing us so much. If we really want the result of better crops, we will have to plant different seeds.' Then Shining Crow sat down."

"Because they had smoked the pipe, the other warriors considered what Shining Crow had said. These words were so different to what they had been taught that it was very difficult for them to remain quiet. I could see the confused and somewhat angry expressions on their faces, so I spoke first."

Standing Bear shifted his weight. "These are the words which I spoke to them. 'We should listen to Shining Crow.' I said. 'There is one story from our ancestors that caused me to wonder what the true story about our wars really is. The story says that our tribe had a Sickness that came every year. When the Others took our land in the valley, the spirits saw our struggles with our new land in the high country and took the Sickness away from us. The spirits then gave the Sickness to the Others.

" I have been pondering this story…and speaking to the Great Spirit. I received an answer in a dream. I saw that when the Great Heat comes there is Sickness in the swamps, and that is why our tribe left the Great Valley. The Others moved into the same spot where we were living because game and fish are plentiful there. The stories of stealing land and of curses were created by the imaginations of warriors who wanted the riches of the Others.'"

Standing Bear continued, "When my talking ended, there was

an explosion of words from many of the warriors. Some warriors thought that I had lost the wisdom of a medicine man because I had perverted the stories of our ancestors. But there were others who listened with their hearts and agreed that these new thoughts of mine might be true. If they were true, then our battles were not battles of honor, but battles of greed. They persuaded the angry ones to listen to Shining Crow's words.

"Shining Crow told the warriors that if the Sickness was in the swamps, we would not want the land back. Because our hate and our anger had not improved our crops or reduced our hunger, we may want to make the Others our brothers instead of our enemies. He said that if we wanted a harvest of peace and plenty, then that was the crop we should plant.

"Again there were many words. These ideas were very different than the traditions of our tribe. Warring against our neighbors had been part of our culture for generations. Much of boyhood was spent in learning to be a great warrior, and if warriors did not have war, what would they do?"

"I want to know, too," Crooked Feather excitedly interrupted. "What would the warriors do?"

Standing Bear smiled. "Shining Crow responded that warriors would always be needed for protection against attack. But if the warriors were not at war, they could be planting more land and hunting for more food so that the tribe would not be hungry every winter."

"That is what I did today," said Crooked Feather proudly. "I planted so our tribe would not go hungry. I am a great warrior."

Running Wolf cleared his throat with impatience. "Who is telling the story?"

The Medicine Man laughed at the boys' enthusiasm and continued. "The warriors and the tribal council met for many evenings discussing the decision that would be best for the tribe. It was not easy to consider changing traditions and beliefs that were created many generations ago. Some felt they would dishonor their ancestors by changing the traditions. However, we have a tribe of good men and good women. I say women because, although they were not in the council, they knew the words being spoken. They persuaded their men that they would like to live without the fear that came each time the warriors went to battle.

"After a moon had passed away, and after many councils, the elders and the warriors of our village decided to change the way that they treated the Others. They asked Shining Crow what they should do. Shining Crow said that he had traveled down to the Great Valley the previous few days to see if the Others were preparing for battle, and he saw that the Sickness was upon them. He said that death was upon the Others in greater numbers than in other years. There was hunger, and there were very few to do the work of the harvest.

"Some of the warriors said that this would be the best time to do battle. They could get their land back if the warriors were sick. Shining Crow reminded them that if the Sickness was truly in the swamps, they did not want the land. Rather than going to battle, they should take food and medicines to the Others and assist them with their harvest.

"There was concern among the council that if we took our food, we would not have enough for ourselves. Shining Crow said to remember the Law of the Harvest. If we were generous to those in need, the Great Spirit would be generous to us. After much discussion, the tribal council decided to do what Shining Crow suggested. Some of the women insisted on going with them to care for the sick."

Running Wolf broke in. "My mother told me that even though she knew that Father was doing a great thing, she was very worried about him. The Others did not know of our change of attitude towards them and might think we were coming to attack. My father volunteered to go into the village first to explain to them our intentions. Mother knew of the anger of the Others and felt deeply that they would not listen to Father. She wanted to go with Father, but I was heavy in her belly. She pleaded with Father not to be the first. He said that this journey was his doing, so he must be the one to take the risk."

Crooked Feather pushed his elbow against the arm of Running Wolf, smiling. "Now who is telling the story?"

Standing Bear smiled and continued, "That is correct, Running Wolf. Shining Crow was worried that if the entire group entered together, the Others would think they were being attacked and fight back in defense. So when our group arrived in the foothills and looked down into the Great Valley, Shining Crow bid the warriors to stop and he went forward alone. However, your mother was correct. The sentry on watch was a young, nervous brave, and when he saw Shining Crow coming towards him with his hand up in salutation, the young man panicked and shot him with an arrow. Our people watched in horror as the sentry pulled Shining Crow into the village. They did not know what to do. I persuaded them to remember that the young man did not know of our intentions, and to let hate and anger go, as Shining Crow had asked. I started a Blessing Chant for Shining Crow and for the Others, and several of the warriors joined in while we waited and watched.

"Shining Crow did not die immediately. He was brought before the Chief, and persuaded the Chief of the Others to listen to his dying words. He told the Chief that our tribe wanted to assist them while they were sick, because we believed that the Sickness was in the swamp. Shining Crow pleaded with the Chief to move their tribe away from the swamp. He told the Chief that our people had brought food and medicine for the Others, and wanted to assist with the harvest. He told the Chief all these things before he died.

"The Chief called together those in the Council that were not sick to decide what to do. Some thought that this was a trick to get our warriors into their village so that we could kill them all, or at least to convince the Others to leave the land so that we could get it back again. But the Chief had seen the eyes of Shining Crow, and had felt of his earnestness and honesty. He wanted to prove that the dying words of Shining Crow were true.

"We waited in the foothills for two hours after Shining Crow was taken. Then we saw the Chief of the Others come out of the Village alone. He walked slowly up to us and greeted us as Brothers. Together, we went into the Village of the Great Valley in peace. We gave them food and medicine, our women nursed their sick, and we helped them move onto higher ground. Then our warriors assisted with the harvest.

"Shining Crow's predictions came true. The harvest was great, and they made us a gift of more food than we had brought to them. All of our warriors except Shining Crow returned to our village, hunting on their return, with more food than our village had known. The Others created a village up in the foothills, but still used the rich earth of the valley to plant in. They planted in the cool of the spring, but avoided the valley as much as possible until the worst of the Great Heat was over. They then harvested the crops. The next summer the Sickness did not come upon the Others, and they brought gifts to us in gratitude, which they have been doing every year since. And our tribe has not gone hungry since that time. We had one year of a poor harvest, but the Others brought extra food and game to assist us through the winter.

"The results of this shift in traditions, thoughts, and beliefs was more than peace with the Others and adequate food for our needs. The neighboring tribes saw our alliance with the Others and were afraid of our strength. These tribes that had done battle with us many times over the passing years would not come up to battle against us any more. We were left alone in complete peace. After a few years, these tribes saw the wealth of our villages and wanted to enter into alliance with us. Now all the tribes in this great area are at peace and growing in prosperity. The results of changing our hearts and planting different seeds have been great indeed."

There was silence in the lodge of Standing Bear. Then Crooked Feather asked quietly, "Does this story mean that no one respects me because I do not respect them?"

"What do you believe, Crooked Feather?" asked the Medicine Man.

Crooked Feather replied, "I feel that the Law of the Harvest says, 'Look to your harvest. If it is not what you want, then look at what you have planted.' I see that I have been planting seeds of disrespect. At least that is what my parents have told me many times, and I admit now that they are correct. But I did not see that these seeds of disrespect were causing others to disrespect me."

"You are a wise man, Crooked Feather," praised the Medicine Man, "because you have opened your heart to learn today. Those who are not wise do not learn. Now take what you have learned and change your heart. It will not be easy because you have made a habit of your hateful words. Keep a remembrance of what results you want, and then slowly your habits will change. Always remember that if you do not like the harvest, look and see what seeds you have planted. I will give you a secret, Crooked Feather. Love is the most powerful seed and the most rewarding harvest."

*   *   *

The washing was complete, and Anne was comfortable in clean sheets and a new nightgown. Grandmother rocked quietly in the rocking chair as Anne contemplated the story that Grandmother had told her.

"Grandmother, is that true for me? Am I making myself sick because of my own thoughts?"

Grandmother smiled as she straightened the covers. "I don't know the answer to that, dear. That answer is inside of you. All I know is that you don't seem to like your harvest. Would you like to do another Dream Picture to see if you can find the seeds you have been planting?"

"Oh yes, Grandmother. I've never really given much thought to what is in my heart. I think I've ignored it for a long time."

*   *   *

Make yourself comfortable, and listen to "Chapter Two—The Law of the Harvest" on Track 2 of CD 1.

Chapter 3

AS A MAN THINKETH, SO IS HE

"Anne, I'm back," whispered John as he sat on the edge of the bed, gently touching the sleeping Anne.

Anne opened her eyes and immediately lifted her arms for a hug. She held John tightly and said, "Oh, John. I'm so glad you're here. I was terrified you'd get stuck again, or lost in the snowstorm."

"George's tractor is strong and steady," said John. "We got to the doctor's and back without any problem." John gently pulled back and looked at Anne. "You don't look as pale as you did this morning."

"Oh, John," said Anne, "Grandmother is amazing. I feel so much better this evening. I'm not sure I still need to see a doctor."

"That's good, because I was dreading having to tell you that the doctor couldn't come," said John. "He was really busy. He seemed to be a caring doctor, but he just couldn't leave his other patients. He said that you were probably in the best hands possible staying with Grandmother."

"She really has helped me more than any doctor I've been to," Anne confirmed, her eyes shining with a new life John had never seen before.

"Even the doctor has great respect for Grandmother," John acknowledged. "He said he wasn't sure what she did but she has taken care of some of his other patients in emergencies, and they have always improved. He was reluctant to give a prescription because he hadn't seen you, but under such unusual circumstances he prescribed some antibiotics and cough syrup. Because of your reactions to antibiotics, he said to use them only if you weren't getting better with whatever Grandmother was doing for you."

"I am getting better," exclaimed Anne. "I'm still coughing, but I hurt less and I have more energy after taking all of Grandmother's magic potions."

Grandmother and George entered the room. "I heard what you

said," laughed Grandmother. "Remember, as White Feather said, this is not magic. This is just Mother Earth giving us her gifts."

"Who is White Feather?" asked John.

"Oh John, Grandmother has been teaching me so much," said Anne. "You have to hear about it all."

"You can talk over dinner," said Grandmother, bringing in a tray. "June sent some food over so you could have some time to be together."

"These people are so kind, Anne," John said. "I still can't believe you all would take absolute strangers into your homes."

Anne started to giggle. "And...it's no secret how strange I can be. Right, honey?"

John felt a renewed hope by Anne's sense of humor, and smiled as he bent to kiss her forehead. "Well, they say like attracts like...so, I guess we're in it together. Listen, I have to go back with George because you are in Grandmother's only extra bed, but George has agreed to stay through dinner so I could spend some time with you. He promised to bring me back in the morning."

"May we call the kids before we eat, Grandmother?" asked Anne. "We have a calling card."

"Certainly, dear. We want those children to know that they are loved and that you are all right." Grandmother and George left the room, and soon Anne and John were on the phone telling all that had happened to them.

A few minutes after John and George left, Grandmother was again working with her herbs. "I would like to put another poultice on your chest to work on your lungs while you are sleeping tonight."

Anne watched Grandmother as she worked. "Grandmother, I've been thinking about that last Dream Picture we did, the one about my harvest. I've been wondering about the seeds I've been planting, which you said were my thoughts. I know now that my thoughts may be part of my problem, but I don't quite know what is wrong with them or how to change them. Can you teach me about my thoughts?"

Grandmother smiled knowingly. She sat next to Anne with a bowl filled with a pasty mixture of herbs. She started gently spreading the paste across Anne's chest. "Tell me, Anne, what are some of your thoughts? First of all, how do you describe your physical symptoms?"

Anne thought for a moment. "Well, when I'm having a bad day and can't get out of bed, I'll tell John, 'My fibromyalgia is acting up today. My pain is so severe that I can't move.'"

"Here are the two problems with those statements," said Grandmother. "First, when you use the word 'my' you're actually owning the problem. You're telling your body that this diagnosis or this pain belongs to you. Because you own this problem, your body responds by keeping the problem as part of you. It often works better if you simply express your experience of the problem, such as 'My muscles are feeling very achy today.' Or 'I feel a lot of pain in my joints today.' This allows you to express what you are experiencing without telling your body to keep that experience because it belongs to you."

"I do use 'my pain' and 'my fatigue' and 'my fibromyalgia' a lot," Anne commented. "I didn't realize I could make myself worse with my words."

Grandmother nodded. "Be careful with owning a diagnosis. I know that many people feel relieved when they can give their symptoms a name. However, when they say 'I have...' and name their diagnosis, that is accepting ownership of that cluster of symptoms that the diagnosis is named after. They are, in reality, telling the body to accept these symptoms as its own and to keep them.

"Letting go of a diagnosis is hard to do in our culture. We use the diagnosis to communicate about our experiences so that others will understand what we are going through. But it may work better for your body if you say, 'I am experiencing the symptoms of fibromyalgia, or diabetes, or breast cancer,' or whatever the diagnosis may be. This allows you to communicate what your symptoms are without telling your body that it must continue to own this set of symptoms."

"That all makes sense," responded Anne thoughtfully. "I was glad when they told me I had fibromyalgia, because then I had a name for the pain. It's a legitimate reason I can give other people for why I can't get out of bed or do my work. Then everyone won't think I'm a hypochondriac or just lazy. Hmm...I just realized how worried I was about what others thought of me."

Grandmother lifted a small cotton towel out of some warm water, wrung out the excess moisture, and put it over the herbs. Then she put a piece of wax paper over the towel to keep the moisture off of Anne's nightgown, while she explained, "Many people judge others' actions when they are sick. It's common for us to want to tell others a diagnosis that will explain our actions so that they won't judge us. It's hard to not care about what others think of us, but it is possible.

"I feel that there is yet another reason why you feel better about having a diagnosis. Could it be that you were also judging yourself harshly because you couldn't do the things you felt you were supposed to do? By accepting the diagnosis as your own, it allowed you to stop judging yourself."

"That's probably true," said Anne. "I was able to let go of some of the guilt I was feeling about not being a good wife and mother. But, it didn't last long. I still often feel that I am worthless because I can't do the things I feel I'm supposed to."

"You just used the second word I was going to talk about: the word 'can't.'" Grandmother stood to clean up while she continued, "When you use the word 'can't' you are telling your body that this is something that is impossible for you to do. Your body believes what your mind tells it, and then responds by worsening until it is truly impossible for you to do that thing. The reality is, Anne, that on the days you are experiencing pain you *can* move, you *can* get out of bed, but at a severe cost. You don't move and don't get out of bed because the increase in pain and fatigue would be difficult to bear. But this is your choice, and not because moving is physically impossible for you. If you had a spinal cord injury and were paralyzed, then your reality may be that it is impossible for you to move. But even then, I would hesitate to use the word 'can't' because you don't know how much healing may take place over the months and years ahead. By using the word 'can't,' you're accepting your limitation as permanent, which signals your body to stop the healing process. It may work better for you to say something like, 'I am experiencing severe pain when I move. I will stay in bed for a time so that I may rest and my body may heal.' By thinking or saying something like this, you are telling your body that you are choosing to take care of it, and that it may begin healing even as you choose to stay in bed.

While Grandmother was making more herbal tea, she continued, "Other negative self-talk that I often hear, and that I have thought and said myself until I learned better, are words like 'I'm not loved.' 'I am so stupid.' 'I'm not appreciated.' 'I'm a bad person.' 'I'm not worthy.' The words 'I am' are a strong force for change. Other attitudes I see are: 'Look at all my sufferings.' 'My family would be better without me.' 'I can't endure this.' 'Everyone treats me badly.' 'I'm afraid I'll never be good enough.'"

"Oh, dear," said Anne. "I've thought most of those."

"That's all right, dear. You're still learning. Don't be afraid of the past. Fear is especially harmful. 'I'm afraid I have cancer.' 'I'm afraid I'm going to die.' 'I'm worried that something is really wrong.' Fear is a very strong emotion, and constant fears and worries, combined with these thoughts and words, may create the very thing that is feared.

"These negative thoughts are mental commands that eventually affect our bodies. 'My life is awful' may be translated by our bodies into 'I am sick.' As our bodies begin to feel the negative energy of our thoughts, they respond by transferring the negativity of our thoughts into our bodies. Our complaints are transferred to physical symptoms, which distract us from our emotional pain. 'Oh, my aches and pains.' 'I am so sick.' 'I wish I could just cut this painful part out.' 'I will never get better.' 'I would rather be dead than feel this way.' Our body continues to respond by becoming or feeling according to the commands that we give it.

"We must be very careful in thinking or saying these words as a statement of fact. The words 'I am' are very powerful. They open the door for our bodies to accept these beliefs as our own. The body often responds with self-fulfilling prophecy."

Grandmother poured some more herbal tea and brought it to Anne. Anne sipped on the tea and felt the warmth throughout her body. "Grandmother, I can see how my thoughts are adding to my misery. But, it seems to be an endless circle. I feel sick so my emotions react, and then the negative thoughts come automatically. How do you stop the reactions?"

Grandmother sat in her rocking chair and started rocking. "There is another story of Running Wolf that my Oma used to tell."

* * *

Running Wolf woke up with a start. Where was he? He did not recognize his surroundings. Then he remembered. He was on his Manhood Quest. Yesterday he had awakened at dawn, full of excitement. His mother had gently dressed him in a new buckskin outfit, braided his hair and applied paint to his face. This was her last act to her boy-son as his mother. Later, when he returned a man, their relationship would be different. Their lodge would become his, and she would be required to respect and obey him as a man.

Yesterday, Running Wolf had eagerly attended the ceremony that sent him and three other boys on their quest. Today, he was not so eager and excited. He felt hungry and cold and was still tired after a night of restless sleep. The young boy-man could not understand why the Great Spirit was making this so hard for him.

During the Manhood Quest Ceremony, Standing Bear had thrown four bones on the ground, one bone for each of the boys. He told the boys that these bones represented the paths they would take toward manhood, and the direction that each bone pointed would be the direction that each boy was to travel on his quest. The bone of Running Wolf had pointed east. East was directly up the mountain. None of the other boys, who had good legs, had been required to climb the mountain.

Running Wolf arose from the ground and carefully climbed onto the outcrop of rock that he had slept under during the night. He sat down, quietly looking down over the mountain valley that he lived in. He carefully reviewed the events of the previous day.

He remembered how determined he had been to show that his will was stronger than his stick leg. He decided to reach the top of the mountain before he stopped for the night. He had climbed slowly but steadily during the previous afternoon, but as the sky began to darken he stumbled over a rock with his lame leg. He fell, landing on another sharp rock, which put a large cut in his good leg. He had to stop and sit down to put pressure on the wound to stop the bleeding.

Running Wolf had been sent on this quest with no food, no medicine pouch, and no tools except a knife and flint. He had looked around to see if there was anything that he could use to bandage his wound with. He saw some stinging nettle and knew there would be lamb's ear nearby. He looked around carefully, and finally found the lamb's ear growing directly under the outcropping of rock he was sitting on. He had picked a couple of large leaves and pressed them to the wound, but did not know how to keep them from falling off of his leg. He looked around and saw a yucca plant that had recently bloomed. The flowers were beautiful and delicate, and the stem was thick and strong. He carefully cut the stem at its base and then cut the flowers off. He pounded the stem with a rock and pulled the fibers out. He braided the stem fibers into a small rope and used it to tie on the lamb's ear. The wound indeed felt better after it was bandaged.

Running Wolf had planned to hike late into the night, but with one lame leg and one wounded leg, he did not have the sure-footedness necessary to travel the treacherous paths in the dark. Resigned, he had sat down dejectedly by the rock, and as the sun vanished from the sky, he had considered his situation.

"Why did the Great Spirit make me climb the mountain? Why is He making my Quest so hard?" he wondered. "Crooked Feather got to travel along the valley. That would have been easier for me. I always travel that way to talk to the animals."

Running Wolf continued to question. "Why did I not look where I was going so that I stumbled and cut myself? Why am I so careless and stupid?"

"I am cursed," he had thought. "Maybe I am being punished for being so proud of my knowledge. Standing Bear has taught me much, and sometimes when I cannot run and play with the others, I like to tell them things I have learned so that they do not feel I am worthless. I have been very proud of my knowledge because it makes me feel important. The Great Spirit must be punishing me for my pride."

"If I did not have this lame leg," Running Wolf had thought, "I would be at the top of the mountain by now. This leg causes me nothing but trouble. It hurts from simply walking, and now my pain is great because of the long climb I have made. Sometimes I wish I could cut it off and replace it with a stick. Then it would never hurt."

Running Wolf continued to think. "I am hungry and thirsty. I should have eaten more of the last meal mother prepared for me as her boy-son. I was too excited to eat much, and I could see that she was disappointed. She encouraged me to eat more to increase my strength for the quest, but I just wanted to get out of there and talk with my friends about what might happen during our Manhood Quest. I am so stupid. I should have eaten more."

"If I had some water," Running Wolf spoke out loud into the increasing darkness of the night, "I could make some nourishing stinging nettle and yucca root soup. But I cannot find water in the dark with two bad legs. I am truly cursed."

Running Wolf found tears running down his face. "I am just a baby," he thought. "I will never be a man. I will never be strong enough to finish my Manhood Quest. I cannot even go half a day without crying." He despondently pulled himself under the out-cropping of rock, curled into a ball for some warmth, and fell into a restless sleep, his face still damp with his tears.

Now it was morning, and Running Wolf was surveying his world from on top of the rock. The sun had not yet shown itself above the mountain behind him, but it was already making colors on the clouds and beginning to lighten the sky. He knew he needed some water and looked around for some plant leaves that he could at least chew on for their moisture. He saw a few succulent plants sparsely spaced on the hillside below, but he did not leave the rock to pluck the leaves just yet. He pulled off the bandage he had applied the night before and examined his wound. It was still very painful, but it did not look as bad as he thought it would. He wanted to keep away the bad spirits that make a wound fill with sickness. He could do this by washing the wound before he bandaged it again, but he needed water to do that.

Running Wolf shivered. He could make a fire to warm himself, but he did not want the villagers to see his smoke and know that he had not yet traveled very far.

Running Wolf remembered that Standing Bear had given many instructions on how to succeed in the Manhood Quest. He tried to remember the things that Standing Bear had told the boys during the Manhood Quest Ceremony. Running Wolf usually listened well to the words of the Medicine Man, but this time he had been so excited to start his quest that he had not listened attentively to the wise man's words. He closed his eyes so he could focus on the words that Standing Bear had given.

Standing Bear had told the boys that the purpose of the Manhood Quest was to obtain a Vision. This Vision would tell them what the purpose of their life was to be; what mission they were to fulfill during the years of their manhood. He said each boy would receive his Vision in a different manner. There was no specific way to obtain the Vision, but each boy would be led in the best way to find it and would know it when they had received it. They were not to return until they had received their Vision.

Standing Bear had said something about thoughts. Yes, that was it. He had said that it was not the strength of their bodies that would allow them to succeed in their quest for manhood. He said that it was the strength of thoughts that makes boys into men. He said to watch carefully the thoughts that they allowed to come into their minds during their journeys. Learning to control these thoughts would bring success to their Manhood Quest and allow them to obtain their Vision.

Running Wolf considered the thoughts he had allowed into his mind. He saw that he had not attempted to control them at all. The thoughts during his climb had been of showing everyone how great he was, in spite of his lame leg, by reaching the top of the mountain before he stopped. His thoughts were centered on what he wanted everyone to think of him rather than what the Great Spirit wanted him to do. His thoughts after his injury had been full of fear and complaints.

Running Wolf felt remorse for his thoughts the night before. The Medicine Man had taught him about the Law of the Harvest. Running Wolf had been taught that his thoughts were the seeds he was planting, and the harvest he received depended on the thoughts he planted. Standing Bear had taught him ways to control his thoughts, and although he was still learning, he had not allowed such negative thoughts into his mind in a long time. He realized now that if he continued thinking this way his Manhood Quest would be long and difficult.

Running Wolf decided to use the technique that Standing Bear had taught him of how to clear his thoughts so that he could better control them. He briefly thought that this was something he should have done yesterday morning instead of talking with the other boys. But he quickly set that thought aside because he knew that he must let go of the past, and be present in the moment, if he wanted to clear his mind.

He sat cross-legged on the rock and, for a moment, contemplated the beauty of the dawn and the little green valley below him. Then he closed his eyes and spoke to the Great Spirit. "Great Spirit, I am grateful for this experience. I know I am here to learn. I know that the lameness of my leg, and the wound I have been given, are part of my learning. I desire to be successful in my Manhood Quest. I desire to receive a Vision of the purpose for which You have created me. Please open my heart and my mind to remember the truths that You have already planted within me. Please teach me today how I am to take the journey of my Quest with the gift of weak and injured legs that You have given me. Thank You for always teaching me."

Running Wolf took several deep breaths to draw in the power of the spirits of the air. He then concentrated on the strength of the rock he was on, and the strength of the mountain beneath the rock, and the power of Mother Earth beneath the mountain. He imagined the power of Mother Earth rising from deep within the center of the mountain and saw in his mind's eye the energy flowing into him. Running Wolf filled himself with the strength and the power of the earth. Then he considered the Light of the Great Spirit that filled the heavens and gave light to the sun and moon and stars. He pictured the Light of the Great Spirit coming down and entering him, filling his entire body. He felt the Light of the Great Spirit mingling with the power of Mother Earth. He was Man, holding his place between the heavens and the earth. He needed the energy of both.

Then Running Wolf focused on his breathing. He felt and listened to his breaths. He did nothing else but feel and listen to his breathing.

Thoughts often entered the mind of Running Wolf while he was going through this process. Thoughts such as "I wonder where Crooked Feather is right now?" or "How am I going to travel with two bad legs?" would come uninvited into his mind. As he recognized that these thoughts were his mind running away from the moment, he pictured the thoughts as a flock of birds and watched them fly away until his mind was clear again. In the beginning he watched many birds fly away, but after some time there were fewer and fewer thoughts that came without his permission.

He felt a change come over his body and his mind. He knew from experience that this feeling was a change in the pattern of his brain energy that allowed him greater access to the knowledge within him. It had taken, in the past, many times of repeating this process to recognize this change, but now he could feel it easily. He felt the feelings in his body that this change brought, the very peaceful feelings, while he continued to keep his mind clear by concentrating on his breathing. Soon he forgot the breathing and sat in stillness.

The word came naturally to his mind. He knew that it was not one of his runaway thoughts. He knew that it came from deep within him, that it was knowledge given to him by the Great Spirit. The word was "Trust." The word filled him with gentle warmth and brought him joy. He knew that all he needed to do was trust in the Great Spirit. He was to trust that the Great Spirit was leading him on this quest, and that what was happening to him was part of the process of obtaining his Vision. All would be well.

Running Wolf took another deep breath and allowed his mind to come back to where he was sitting. He slowly opened his eyes. He felt at peace. He knew that all was as it should be, and he trusted that he would be led to the next important step in his Quest.

Running Wolf saw movement out of the corner of his eye. A beaver! What was a beaver doing this high on the mountain? There must be water nearby.

Running Wolf knew he was not fast enough to follow the beaver, so he patiently watched the direction the beaver traveled until it disappeared. Then he climbed down from the rock and put another leaf on the wound as a bandage. He cut and gathered some leaves of the yucca plant and dug out the root with his knife. He picked more leaves of the lamb's ear, put all the plants in his pouch, and set off slowly in the direction where the beaver had disappeared. He left the main path and found himself on a small game trail.

After traveling for a time, Running Wolf came to a cleft in the mountainside. He heard running water. As he entered the cleft, the sound of water became very loud, echoing off the walls. Traveling a short distance, he entered a widening in the cleft and entered a small canyon. A waterfall was flowing about thirty feet down the back of the canyon wall, forming a small pool at the base. The beaver was in the pool and had built a large den to the side. There was no stream coming from the pool, so Running Wolf decided it must empty into a cavern in the mountain below. He wondered if this was the source of the spring that came out of the edge of the mountain near their village and fed the clear stream that flowed by their lodges.

This small canyon hidden away in the mountain was exquisitely beautiful. Plants and flowers were hanging on the sides of the canyon wall, drinking in the mist of the waterfall. It looked like the Spirit of the Water had planted a hanging garden for Her pleasure. Several cedar trees were growing around the pool's edge. An area to the left was filled with blackberry bushes. The floor of the canyon was carpeted with grass and wildflowers. The canyon was a feast for the eyes.

Running Wolf took in the beauty, and then set to cleaning his wound. He found a bowl-shaped piece of bark nearby and filled it with water. He cut up one of the leaves of the yucca plant, pounded the pieces with a rock, and then put them into the water, squeezing them with his hands. A soapy substance formed in the water, and Running Wolf used the soapy water to clean his wound. It was painful, but he knew it was necessary to keep bad spirits out of the wound. He then put his leg under the small waterfall and let the clear water rinse and cleanse the wound. He opened another leaf and laid the inner side of the yucca against the wound to reduce inflammation, and again tied the small rope around the leaf, securing it to his leg. He felt better knowing that now his leg was safe from the bad spirits that make a wound fill with sickness.

Running Wolf found some dead twigs and branches under the trees. He gathered them and tore the fiber from the bark of one of the larger pieces. He placed the fiber in a small pile on an old log and added to it some pith from the yucca stem. Using his flint and knife, he was able to start a small fire. The warmth of the fire felt good. After warming himself, he looked for plants that he could use for food. He found bushes ripe with blackberries and quickly picked the juicy fruit. He popped several berries into his mouth to ease his hunger pangs. He picked more, filling a large leaf he had picked from a plant nearby. He brought them back and laid them next to the fire by the pond.

Running Wolf continued to search around the clearing and found bulrush, cattail plants, and other plants that had roots that were good to eat. His mother used many of these roots to give flavor and substance to the buffalo and venison stews she cooked in the large black pot near the lodge's entrance. Running Wolf pulled up the rootstalks and some of the young shoots. He found more nettle, and using a large lamb's ear leaf as a glove, carefully cut a stalk full of leaves. He built a tripod out of sticks over the fire and placed the bark bowl full of water just above the flames. He cut up some of the roots and shoots he had found, along with some of the yucca root, and placed the slices and a handful of nettle into the boiling water. Soon Running Wolf had a nutritious soup. It was not the best-tasting meal he had ever had, but as he was eating more berries after finishing his soup, he felt very satisfied.

Running Wolf lay down by the fire and looked up at the beautiful little waterfall. He looked around at the lush growth in this little canyon. Here was a place of peace and beauty hidden away from the world. Here was a place that animals came to drink and eat, animals that could teach him. Running Wolf realized that if he had not stumbled and cut himself when he did, he would never have found this little canyon. Running Wolf knew that he did not need to reach the top of the mountain to find his Vision. He knew that his schoolroom was right here, in this beautiful little canyon, not very far from the valley floor. He knew from the depths of his heart that this was where he would find his Vision.

"Thank You, Great Spirit, for pointing the bone in this direction. Thank You for the wound in my leg that made me stop in the exact place that would allow me to find this canyon, because my thoughts and my heart were not listening to You at the time. Thank you for teaching me the importance of controlling my thoughts and the importance of keeping negative thoughts away. Thank You for the beauty of this teaching place that you have led me to. I trust that You will continue to lead me in each step of my quest until I find my Vision." Then Running Wolf fell into a restful sleep, warmed by the fire and the peace in his heart.

* * *

W ait! You can't stop the story there. Aren't you going to tell me what Running Wolf's Vision was?" pleaded Anne as Grandmother stood up to stretch her legs.

Grandmother laughed. "Honey, that is another story for another time."

"Well," said Anne, leaning back and crossing her arms over her chest, a twinkle in her eyes. "I'm not leaving this bed until I hear the complete story. So, Grandmother, you decide how long you want me taking up your spare bedroom."

Grandmother chuckled and tucked the quilt around Anne's legs. "Stay as long as you like, but I'll put you to work when you recover. But tonight it is late and you must rest. However, to assist you in relaxing tonight, I'll go through one more Dream Picture with you. This is a Dream Picture that will assist you in learning how to control your thoughts through meditation. Meditation allows the body to relax to the point where healing can take place much faster. It has been proven to lower blood pressure and reduce the effects of stress on the body.

"I like to use meditation to reach the point where I can follow the admonition of Psalms 46, which says, 'Be still, and know that I am God.' I often use meditation as the listening part of my prayers. I feel the love of God and frequently receive answers to questions when I am meditating.

"Meditation has assisted me in discovering my negative thoughts and beliefs and in controlling what thoughts I let into my mind. I have found that by acknowledging what my deepest thoughts, feelings and beliefs are, I am able to uncover the reasons my body, and even my life, is in its current state. Whether healthy or ill, happy or sad, fulfilled or empty, I know that it is all an accumulation of my own thoughts and beliefs. We can choose to change any of our negative thoughts and beliefs into something positive. We can then find healing by filling our minds and hearts with thoughts of faith, love, peace and joy. This is done through deep self-reflection, constant prayer and effort, and a true desire to believe that we can change. Our thoughts can lift and improve, and at times even cure our physical ailments."

"But, Grandmother," Anne protested. "I can't tell you how many times I've wished and prayed to be healthy again."

"Remember," Grandmother interceded, "that controlling our thoughts is an ongoing process. We lead busy lives, full of constant distractions. Even great teachers, monks and religious leaders go into seclusion to be able to focus. Remember that Jesus went into the wilderness for forty days before He began His ministry.

"Most of us have let idle thoughts have their own will for most of our lives. Many thoughts have become habitual. It may be difficult to change a habitual thought pattern. Rarely can we force it away, or it will return again and again. All we can do is accept it, dismiss it, and let it go. Then we can replace it with a positive thought. As we purposely think positive thoughts, the negative thoughts will come less and less often.

"If you aren't successful with this Dream Picture in the way you think you should be, do not be discouraged. Controlling our thoughts takes practice. You can follow this process again and again."

*   *   *

Make yourself comfortable, and listen to "Chapter 3—As A Man Thinketh, So Is He" on Track 3 of CD 1.

Chapter 4

EMOTIONS AND ILLNESS— LETTING THE POISON OUT

A nne awakened early and sat up in bed, stretching her arms above her head. She could tell she was getting better. She smiled, swinging her feet to the floor and padding over to the mirror on the door. She was definitely well enough to know she looked like a mess. All she wanted now was to wash up, run a brush through her hair, and put a toothbrush to work.

Grandmother, hearing her up, came in the room with a fresh towel and suggested that Anne take a hot bath. "We don't have any fancy bath oils," Grandmother shrugged, "but there's a carton of Epson salts and a squeeze bottle of dish soap on the shelf."

Thirty minutes later, as Anne climbed out of the bathtub, she felt tired again and gratefully slipped back into bed as Grandmother arrived with breakfast.

"June called while you were in the tub," Grandmother said. "Apparently John insisted on helping with the chores this morning so George has him milking cows, slopping pigs and gathering eggs."

"John milking cows? I can't believe it!" laughed Anne.

"June's getting a big kick out of it, too. Anyway, George said they wouldn't be done with the chores until around eleven and he would bring John over as soon as they were finished."

Anne shook her head. "I wish I was there to see it. I can't imagine John spending his time with pigs and chickens. He hates to change the water in the kids' goldfish bowl."

Grandmother laughed. "Country air gets in the blood real quick. If he's here much longer, he'll be considering buying a farm."

Grandmother started humming as she prepared Anne's morning dose of herbal tea. "You are improving, so I am changing the formula a bit. This may taste a little better than the last. I've taken out the cayenne pepper, and added some lemon and orange rind, along with some peppermint to improve your digestion as you are healing."

Anne watched Grandmother as she worked. "You always seem so happy, Grandmother. What's your secret?"

"There's no secret to happiness, dear," Grandmother said, turning to look at Anne. "I have difficult things happen to me, just like everyone else, but I have learned over the years that I can choose how I want to feel, no matter what is happening. 'A merry heart doeth good like medicine; but a broken spirit drieth the bones.' That's in Proverbs." She turned back to her work.

Anne set aside her breakfast tray. "In the Dream Picture about the harvest, you said our emotions are like the water and the sun that feed the seeds. You said thoughts with strong emotions are a powerful creative force. I'm worried that my feelings of depression are so strong I'll never be able to get better."

Grandmother gave a compassionate "hmm" as she continued her work.

"I know how good I have it, Grandmother. My husband is really wonderful. My kids are sweet and loving despite their problems. I have much more than other people. I should be happy. I don't know why I get so depressed. I know my depression makes my body feel worse because I always hurt more. I would like to be like you and choose to be happy, but I don't know how."

Grandmother brought the tea over to Anne. She sat again in the rocking chair. "You say you don't know why you're depressed. That's the problem, honey. You can't let go of the depression until you find the cause. There is always a cause."

Anne sipped on the tea. Grandmother was right. It did taste better and was much easier to drink. "The doctors tell me the cause of my depression is a chemical imbalance and there is nothing I can do but take medication. With antidepressant medication I can accomplish more. I am definitely less irritable, and my family seems to like me better. But then I feel like a flat 'Stepford wife,' like I've lost the real me. The drugs keep me from feeling much of anything.

"If I don't take anything I feel like I am falling down a dark hole and I have to fight to climb out. It's exhausting, to say the least. The medications do keep me from feeling like I am so deep in the hole, but sometimes I see myself far, far away in the distance, still trying to climb out. When I started getting so many side effects from the medicines, I was almost grateful to stop them."

"Medicine for depression can be a life-saver in an emergency," responded Grandmother, "just as a tourniquet can stop heavy bleeding from an artery. But the tourniquet does not cure the cause of the bleeding. It simply stops all blood from entering and leaving the area, which can cause damage in the long run. The cure comes by repairing the artery. A person with depression often experiences a chemical imbalance. However, I believe that often the chemical imbalance is created by negative thoughts, beliefs and emotions formed by past experiences and buried deep in the subconscious. Anti-depressant medication may help the chemical imbalance, but it does not cure the depression. The cure comes only by finding and fixing the cause of the depression. Depression often comes with physical problems such as hormonal imbalances, protracted pain and prolonged illness, but I believe the root cause is most often a feeling of having no control over your life and not being able to live as the person you really are. Remember when I asked you, 'Who are you?' Who did you eventually find yourself to be, once you removed all the problems and weaknesses of your earth-life?"

"I remember seeing myself as full of light, with light radiating far out from me. I saw how powerful I was and how much love was in me. That was an amazing experience!"

"How is that different from what you usually feel?" Grandmother asked.

"While I've been sick, I've felt dark and weak. You're right. I often feel I have no control over my life, like I'm trapped in this dark hole with no hope it will ever get better. I'm actually a very different person than I thought I was. I've been living my life as a limited version of myself."

Anne continued pondering as she finished drinking the tea. Grandmother started rocking and closed her eyes. Anne smiled. She was beginning to recognize Grandmother's storytelling expression. Grandmother spoke. "It is time to tell you, Anne, about Oma's story."

*   *   *

Oma's name, before she became Oma, was Katherine. Katherine married at nineteen years of age, and by the time she was twenty-five, she had three children. That was when she became sick. The doctors said something was wrong with her liver, but couldn't tell her more than that. She was nauseated all the time and very tired. At times she would get yellow eyes. The doctors did not have any medicines to help her. They told her that she would continue to get worse, and that eventually her liver would fail and she would die. However, Katherine was familiar with herbs and homeopathics to heal the liver. While these remedies kept her from getting a lot worse, she did not get better.

After several years of illness and another pregnancy which almost killed her, Katherine found herself in bed most of the time because of the severe fatigue and nausea that was now a constant part of her life. She had a family of four children to raise and a farm that required as much of her time as it did of her husband, but she was unable to do what needed to be done. She fell into a deep depression, or melancholy, as they called it in those days.

Katherine was a religious woman. Her family had joined the Latter-day Saint church in Germany and came to Utah because of their religion. As she started sinking further and further into the dark hole, as you called it, she turned desperately to God. As she was in bed most of the time, she spent hours reading the Bible and the Mormon scriptures, and prayed often as she was reading. When she had the strength, she would go to the Mormon temple to contemplate and seek answers to her problems.

After several months of living like this, Katherine had a dream. In the dream she was a little girl. She was playing in the yard of their small log cabin and her father came up to her. Her father handed her a piece of chocolate. Candy was very rare when she was a child, and Katherine loved chocolate, but something about this piece of candy made her hesitate to take it. Her father insisted that she take it, and as she was an obedient girl, she took it and reluctantly ate it. The chocolate tasted good at first, but as she began to chew it, there was a terrible, bitter taste inside. She saw that inside of the chocolate was a black fluid that was a slow poison. She saw the black poison go inside of her body and stay there because there was no way for it to leave. She watched in her dream as the poison slowly moved from place to place in her body as she grew up, until it lodged in her liver.

Katherine woke from the dream very perplexed. The memory of the dream was clear, and she felt there was a message in it. However, she knew that her father loved her and that he would never give her poison.

Katherine reflected back on her childhood. Her parents were German, and by tradition, German fathers were strict and stern. Her father was overbearingly strict and stern, just as his father had been before him. He used a loud voice, harsh criticism and a willow stick, if necessary, to keep his children in line. Katherine had watched her older brother Wilhelm receive harsh beatings several times a year. She decided that she would never receive a beating, because, unlike her brother, she would be very obedient.

Katherine loved her father. There was sometimes a gentle side to him, and at times he would set her on his lap and tell stories of his own childhood. She knew that he loved her and the other children and was doing what he thought was best for them. But it was not often easy to see this gentle and loving side of him. Because of her father's anger, her brother Wil had run away from home when he was seventeen and had not been heard from again.

Katherine remembered that she had tried hard to be obedient and to please her father. She felt that if she were just good enough, he might show love to her more often. But as he became busier each day farming the sandy soil, digging irrigation ditches, and striving to keep his family alive, he became more irritable, and the gentle times came few and far between. He never beat her as he did Wil, but his words were often critical and unkind.

Katherine remembered a time when she was about nine years old. She had been given the job of cleaning the wooden kitchen floor, which meant sweeping away the sandy soil tracked in from the farm and then scrubbing the floor with a wet, soapy brush. After rinsing the floor and allowing it to dry, she had to apply a paste wax, rubbing it into the wood with a soft cloth until it had a beautiful shine. Katherine had helped her mother clean the floor before, but had never done it all by herself. She worked very hard all day on the floor and was excited for her father to return home and see what she had accomplished.

When her father came home, she could tell that he was in a bad mood. He angrily told her mother that he had discovered that their hired hand had been stealing from them. He had spent the afternoon at the sheriff's office. This was time that could have been better spent harvesting. After dinner, he started the nightly ritual of checking on the children's chores. Katherine hoped her work on the kitchen floor would make him feel better. But when he saw it, he said irritably, "The wax is smudgy and uneven. You need to apply the wax more evenly and keep rubbing until the entire floor sparkles. This is an awful job."

Katherine remembered that she had run to her room in tears. She felt like her heart was broken. She sobbed on her bed for a long time. And then she remembered that it was at this time that her heart turned numb. She knew her father was having a difficult time, so she decided that she would simply not let this bother her. She would obey and please her father. So she went down and spent the night rubbing the floor with a soft cloth until it sparkled evenly. No longer would she expect any kind words from him. No longer would she yearn in her heart for his love.

Katherine reflected on this childhood incident for a long time. Tears surfaced unbidden as she felt the pain that her little nine-year-old heart had experienced because of feeling rejected by her father. She began to sob in her pillow, feeling the pain in a heart that had long been numb from feeling anything.

Katherine suddenly realized that it was this numbing feeling of her heart that caused her to experience a physical numbness. This numbness would spread throughout her entire body and would last for several days. These symptoms had terrified her because she thought she was having a stroke. The doctors examined her time and again, but they never could find a problem. After several episodes of this numbness they gave up trying to find the cause. One doctor had told her she was a hypochondriac, and she had wondered if he was right. Now, at last, she was beginning to understand what was happening. Her body was responding to the numbness of her heart.

As Katherine's tears continued, she further contemplated this incident and many other similar incidents in her life. She realized that within the pain that her heart was feeling, there was also anger. She felt anger towards her father. This realization concerned her because she felt that she had previously forgiven her father—that she had let go of all of his anger against her. However, Katherine's own anger towards him now came forth stronger than she had ever felt it before. She now opened the door to this anger and it came flooding out. Within the quiet protection of her room, she cried a deep, yearning cry.

"Papa, why did you have to be so angry? Why did you beat Wil and make me fear you? Why did you criticize me no matter what I did? Why didn't you recognize the normal weaknesses of children? Why couldn't you show me any love?" She continued this way for quite some time until the anger was finally spent, and she lay exhausted on her bed.

Katherine was surprised to discover that besides feeling exhausted, she also felt lighter. She felt different somehow. She realized that the numbness in her heart was also less.

Another incident from Katherine's past came clearly to her mind. When Katherine was very young, her family had just arrived in Utah. They settled in a remote area and had no food for the winter, so the Indians took the family into the tribe to winter with them while sharing their store of food. Katherine remembered that as spring came, the Indians started looking for young, tender green plants and roots that might be available to eat. Katherine and Wil, being hungry themselves, also looked for the plants. As they wandered together across the hillside, they found some plants that looked like the ones the Indians were using and happily started chewing on the tender shoots to curb their hunger. When the Indians saw what they were eating, they grabbed the plants and threw them away from the children. These plants were poisonous. The medicine man said the poison must come out or it would kill them. He gave them some bitter herbs to make them vomit.

Katherine now began to consider her dream. As she pondered, the meaning of the dream became clear. The chocolate represented the method of disciplining children that her father had learned. Stern or harsh discipline was believed to be good for children so they would be obedient and hard working. It appeared to be a good method on the outside, but on the inside, under all the logical reasons for it, was the poison of anger, handed down from generation to generation. Katherine saw that as a child, she felt punishment only as her father's anger, and not as the love that it was supposedly based on. She absorbed her father's anger until it became part of her. She had no way to get it out of her. Because she was an "obedient" girl she swallowed her own anger at being treated unfairly. As an adult she no longer remembered it was there. The anger slowly poisoned her body until it settled in her liver where it was now gradually killing her.

Katherine pondered this new revelation. Her father died of a heart attack several years earlier at the age of fifty-nine. Was that the result of unresolved anger towards his own father? Was the anger her father displayed actually the anger from his father, a poison passed down from generation to generation? She wondered about her brother, Wil. She wondered if running away from the anger allowed him to let go of the poison, or if it was still deep within him. She wondered about her younger brothers and sisters, if they had also been poisoned.

From that moment on, Katherine started a different healing regimen. Every day, besides eating healthy foods and taking the herbs to cleanse her liver, she spent some time in the privacy of her room reflecting on the experiences of her life. If the memory of an incident triggered any emotion, she opened her heart and felt all the emotion of that incident. Many things that she had forgotten came forward. Many faces that she thought she had forgiven reappeared in her memory. She learned that forgiveness is a process of letting go. She realized that she still carried unresolved emotions about people she believed she had forgiven years ago. She found that the only way to free herself from the poison of negative emotions was to face them head on. Though it was painful, it was less and less frightening as she let herself experience her emotions truthfully. She began learning more about life and the purpose of each of these difficult experiences. She could now see each incident with more clarity.

There were times when the same incident came up more than once. She learned that there were different levels of emotions that needed to be released. She found that it was all right if the same incident came up again and again because there were more lessons to be learned at each level of the experience.

Slowly Katherine started to improve. She occasionally had a bad day, but she learned that a bad day was a sign that something needed to change. Each "bad day" was a learning experience holding a unique message. One day it might be an awareness that she was taking more herbs than she needed as her body was improving. On another it might be that her body was directing her to eat more vegetables. Once, after several bad days, she discovered that she was feeling much worse because she was upset that one of her children was constantly disobeying (it took her several weeks to work through that one). Another bad day led her to see that she was fearful about finances instead of trusting that God would take care of her, as she and her husband were doing all they could do. Rather than fearing the symptoms of her illness, she chose to feel them all: the depression, fatigue and nausea. She desired to learn the lessons her body had to teach her, and, indeed, with each bad day came an incredible lesson.

After one bad day, when Katherine filled her bedside bowl with vomit and became weak with dehydration, she decided that she would like to learn differently. She began to pay more attention to her feelings so that the feelings didn't have to affect her body in order for her to receive the message. As she learned to tune into her heart and listen, her bad days became less and less frequent.

As the anger towards her father came out, Katherine was finally able to let go of it. In her mind, Katherine took the anger that she had felt from him for so many years and gave it back to him. She no longer needed to carry it. She was able, over time, to recognize all that she had learned from her father, from both his strengths and his weaknesses. She began to feel a deep and truly forgiving love for him. She also let go of blaming her father and others for her problems. She had to accept that she had allowed their reactions to affect her. Most importantly, she learned to love herself despite her weaknesses. Because she finally loved herself, everyone else seemed different to her. She was able to stop judging her husband and children and love them more completely than she ever had before.

Within three months, Katherine was back on her feet again, able to accomplish some of her work. The worst of her depression had lifted. Within six months her energy was almost back to normal. Within a year, Katherine felt like a new woman. She was able to feel the feelings of her heart and let them go, rather than stuff them deep inside of her. She was able to listen to the wisdom her heart had to give her and learn from it. She knew that the difficult times were a necessary part of life. Katherine went on to have two more children and continued to live in good health.

Several years after Katherine's miraculous recovery, her brother Wilhelm appeared at her door. He had cancer and had to stop his blacksmith work. The doctors had given him six months to live. His wife had left him several years earlier because of his abusive temper and had taken the children with her. He couldn't work any more and had no place to stay.

Though she had a full house, Katherine welcomed him into her home. She sat with him late into the evening, telling the story of her own illness. She told him of her dream, and reminded him of when they were children and ate the poisonous plants.

Katherine moved over to sit beside her brother on the couch. "I think that you, too, are carrying the poison of anger," she said, putting her arm around his drooping shoulders. "I'm living proof that you can get rid of it. Are you willing to learn?"

Wil said he was not sure he wanted to continue living. "Life has been nothing but pain and heartache," he said. "However, if I could be as happy as you are, it might be worth a try."

Katherine did not quite know how to teach her brother what she had learned by simply listening to her heart. Then she remembered some of the stories the Indians used to tell when she was a child. She made up the stories of Running Wolf, weaving some of the Indian stories with some of her own. With all of these stories she taught Wil the lessons she had learned during her healing process. Listening to these stories, Wil began to understand why he acted the way he did, and where his problems were stemming from, but he found it hard to change his thoughts, beliefs and emotions after so many years and experiences.

Katherine considered how she could reach her brother's heart. She remembered that the turning point in her own healing had been her miraculous dream. She thought that if she could assist Wil in reaching a dream-like state, she might be able to assist him in reaching his own feelings and the knowledge contained within his heart. That is when she made up what she called the Dream Pictures. She used the Dream Pictures with Wil, and he was finally able to make a shift deep within his heart. He was able to begin to feel and let go of the anger and many of the other emotions that he had buried deep inside his body for many years.

Katherine made sure he was eating good food and using the healing remedies. To the amazement of the doctors, they discovered Wil's cancer was in remission. As his health improved, he started helping around the farm, and he even started doing a little blacksmithing again. He was able to visit his children and heal the pain between them, and they came to Utah one summer to stay with him. He lived five years longer than the doctors expected, finally experiencing a productive and happy life.

*   *   *

Grandmother stopped rocking and sat still with a look of child-like nostalgia on her face. "Oma told me all of this when I was a little girl. I loved her stories and learned them well. I would listen to them again and again when she would visit the sick. As I grew older, I found that the Dream Pictures were useful in dealing with my own problems. I would use them time and again to work through different challenges that appeared in my own life. My Oma taught me to consider my emotions as natural and normal. Emotions are only bad when I use them to hurt others or when I push them down and bury them. But I have learned that emotions are just emotions, neither good nor bad. Emotions are a natural part of us and serve a purpose. I can feel them, learn what they have to teach me, and then let them go. Because I do not cloud my mind and my judgment with buried emotions, I can choose to love and be happy in whatever circumstance I am in. It really is just as simple as that!"

Anne's cheeks were damp with tears. "Oh, Grandmother, you were so fortunate to have an Oma in you life. Think about how much you learned from her, and she's still helping people through you. Look how much my life has changed because of you!"

Grandmother smiled. "I'm not doing the changing, dear, you are. I just tell Oma's stories and Dream Pictures."

"Well, I would never know those stories without you. So take a little credit, please!"

"That's not my way," Grandmother said with a wink. "I always pay up front. Credit can be dangerous."

"Okay, okay," Anne laughed. "But right now I'd love to hear another of your wonderful Dream Pictures. Charge it, please."

*   *   *

Make yourself comfortable and listen to "Chapter 4—Emotions and Illness," on Track 1 of CD 2.

Chapter 5

THE MEANING OF ILLNESS
AND ADVERSITY

It had been a long time since Anne had seen such exuberance from John as he bounded to the bedside with wind-burned cheeks and hair full of electricity from pulling off a woolen cap. He kissed her. "How are you feeling today, Anne?"

Anne smiled in return. "I feel tired and achy, but I'm coughing less and my lungs don't hurt. Grandmother is keeping my mind occupied with all her wonderful stories. But look at you! Who is this farmhand and what have you done with my husband?"

John laughed as he ran his fingers through his unkempt hair. "I had a great morning. It feels good to get out and do a little physical labor. Though it sure is cold out there!" John looked back over his shoulder. "How do you do it day after freezing day, George?"

George, shifting his tall frame in the doorway, answered shyly, "I just do it. It's what I've always done. I'd better git on home now. June has lunch waiting."

John stepped over to George and shook his hand. "I want to thank you, George, for all you and June have been doing for Anne and me. You really stepped up and rescued us."

"Just doin' what anyone would. I'll pick ya' up about eight tonight." George ducked out the door.

"What great people. I'd like to be more like them." John laughed as he sat on the end of the bed. "I've been talking George's head off, and he quietly answers with his simple platitudes of wisdom. We fed the pigs—those things are huge! He told me that marriage was like a couple of pigs rolling in the mud together and learning to like it. I laughed at the time, but later saw the wisdom in what he was saying. I could listen to him all day, except that he doesn't say enough to fill ten minutes."

"I know what you mean," smiled Anne, shifting to find a comfortable position while straightening the quilt around her. "I am beginning to see life with very different eyes. I've spent only a day and a half with Grandmother, and my depression is pretty much gone."

John smiled again. "Okay, who is this smiling woman and what have you done with my wife?"

Anne laughed for a moment and then winced in pain. "Ouch! My neck is really hurting. I just wish I could learn how to stop it. Now that my lungs are improving I am feeling the fibromyalgia pain more."

John stood up and muttered, "Well, something is always wrong."

Anne felt a sudden pang of disappointment, but decided to ignore the remark. She knew that John had tried to understand, but she also knew that he had no clue as to what she was going through. "John, I know how much you do for me and I appreciate it. Grandmother pointed out that I may be holding on to beliefs or thoughts that make my physical symptoms worse. Does that make sense?"

"Well, we've often hoped that each treatment would make you better, but nothing we've ever done has worked more than a short time. I don't understand that."

Anne sighed. "John, let's not rehash this argument again. I was just trying to tell you that I am learning some very good reasons why I never get better."

"'Try' is another word that doesn't work, dear," said Grandmother as she appeared in the doorway. "I didn't mean to eavesdrop, but I was coming to tell you that lunch is on the kitchen table. Do you feel ready to eat in the kitchen, Anne? It would be good for your lungs if you got out of bed and sat upright for a while."

Anne carefully sat up, swung her feet to the floor, and put on her slippers. John assisted her into her robe, and they both followed Grandmother into the kitchen. The kitchen was a cheery room with flowered wallpaper, yellow curtains, white cabinets, and the rich aroma of chicken stew.

"When did you find time to make this?" Anne asked with surprise.

"In the country roosters work as a wake-up call," Grandmother said, putting fresh carrot sticks on the table. "Mine tells me my day starts at 5:30."

"That's what time I was out the door this morning, too," John chimed in. "So…I'm fresh-air hungry!"

They slipped into the wooden chairs around the table, and Grandmother, in simple humility, blessed the food. "Our dear Father in Heaven, thank you for the abundance of food that always fills this table. Thank you for sending this wonderful couple to bless my life. Bless the food we are eating this day with Thy Grace. Especially bless Anne with nutrients to heal her body and wisdom to heal her soul. This we ask in Jesus' name, Amen."

"Thank you, Grandmother, that was lovely," said Anne quietly, as John filled her bowl with stew.

John added on, "I don't know how we are blessing your life. I think it's the other way around."

Grandmother smiled with a twinkle in her eye. "Someday, John, you will come to know the incredible blessings of the Law of the Harvest. I reap what I sow. I always welcome an opportunity to serve. It comes back to me tenfold."

"I can't remember tasting anything as good as this stew," exclaimed Anne.

"There is nothing like a newly returned appetite to improve the taste of food," laughed Grandmother.

"Grandmother's stories are so fascinating, John. I can't wait to tell them to you and the children. They'll assist our entire family. By the way, Grandmother," Anne asked, "why did you say the word 'try' doesn't work? My own grandmother always taught me, 'If at first you don't succeed, try, try again.'"

"The word 'try' means 'to make an attempt.' It doesn't mean 'to make a successful attempt,'" replied Grandmother. "In fact, the word itself implies failure. If I 'try' to do something and I do it, I'm not trying, I'm doing. If I 'try' to do something I don't actually do it, I just continue in my efforts to do it. Generally when I use the word 'try,' it gives me a reason for not having succeeded at something.

"I would rather use the phrase, 'If at first you don't succeed, do it a different way.' If what I do doesn't succeed the first time I do it, why would I succeed the next time if I do it the very same way?"

"I read a similar quote in our company newsletter," John said. "The definition of insanity is to do the same thing over and over again and expect different results."

Grandmother laughed. "Exactly. If I keep doing the same thing again and again, I will get the same result again and again. If I do it a different way, I get a different result. That result may still not be what I want, so I do it a third time, a different way than the previous two. I keep finding different ways to do things until I find a way that works. I know that 'trying' doesn't work."

"That makes a lot of sense," said John thoughtfully. "I guess I've 'tried' for years to make Anne be well, and then I get upset that she isn't."

"And then I get upset and 'try' to get John to understand how awful I feel no matter what I do," said Anne. "But I don't know what else to do."

"Thinking that there is only one way to do something is a limiting belief that you have learned to accept, Anne," said Grandmother. "There are always an infinite number of possibilities and choices to make. We just need to believe that they exist and then start seeking them. You will be surprised at how the different choices will come flowing into your hearts."

"Well, then," John started tentatively, "we've sought many different solutions to Anne's illness. We've tried countless choices, as you call them, but still nothing works. A couple of our doctors think Anne is just a hypochondriac. I can see her pain is real, but sometimes I wonder if she is just making herself sick for the attention it gives her."

"I wondered how long it would take for you to say that out loud," said Anne, obviously hurt. "I always thought that's how you felt."

John went on, spilling out his own frustrations to Grandmother. "And if she really is as sick as she claims, why does God allow it? Why won't He stop the pain and hurt and give me back my wife? I've begged and begged Him to let her heal."

"I know how you feel," Grandmother spoke in a soothing voice. "Life is full of mysteries, and right now you both want to comprehend the mystery of illness. At a time when I had many questions, I found this passage in the Bible:

"'To every thing there is a season, and a time to every purpose under the heaven: A time to be born, and a time to die; a time to plant, and a time to pluck up that which is planted; a time to kill, and a time to heal; a time to break down, and a time to build up;

a time to weep, and a time to laugh; a time to mourn, and a time to dance…'

"There is a purpose for everything. We must trust that there is a purpose for Anne being sick, and there is a purpose for the difficulty of your life, John, in caring for her."

John searched Grandmother's clear blue eyes. "Then what is the reason for Anne's suffering, Grandmother?"

"I don't know the reason. I only know there is one," answered Grandmother, standing to clear the dishes. "You may or may not ever find the purpose of Anne's illness and your role in it, but I would guarantee that there is a purpose."

Grandmother noticed John shake his head in confusion. "Let's clean up these dishes and go into the parlor, and then I will tell you a story about Running Wolf, the young Indian friend whom I have already introduced to Anne. Last night we left him on the mountainside, in a small, beautiful canyon, on his Manhood Vision Quest. He has a lame leg that he was born with, and he is now about twelve years old in this story."

* * *

Running Wolf sat by the edge of the deep emerald pool. His legs ached, but he didn't move. The morning sun was radiating down through the small opening above the vermilion cliff canyon, causing the waterfall to spray rainbows into the air. Running Wolf was doing what he did best, quietly watching and listening to the animals, especially the perpetual motion of the beaver family. The parents were working hard, chewing and snipping branches to repair and build onto their home. The three small kits played games chasing each other out of the water and then sliding back down the short muddy bank and disappearing below the surface with a splash. Running Wolf was delighted with their play. The beaver kits were little balls of fur, no larger than a small rabbit. He watched as they swam in and out of the den, splashing and peeking out of the water to look around, and then leaving the pond to pick up small sticks in imitation of their parents.

Running Wolf heard the muffled sound of distant thunder. He looked up at the small patch of sky, clear turquoise above the red cliffs. There was not a cloud in sight. "Maybe there is a storm across the valley," he thought. He caught a movement hovering near the edge of a high cliff. It was a large hawk, also watching the beaver family.

"You had better be cautious, little ones," Running Wolf spoke with his heart to the small beaver kits. "That hawk would like to take you home to his family for dinner." But either the kits did not understand him, or they were just too busy playing to listen. One of the kits swam quickly to the edge and started climbing out. A sharp, cracking noise rang across the pond as the father beaver slapped the water with his tail in warning. The danger signal was too late. The hawk had the young one in his talons, and Running Wolf heard the squeals of the kit echoing off the canyon wall as the hawk climbed into the sky. The other beavers disappeared, and the canyon was quiet once again except for the cascade of water splashing the pool.

Running Wolf stood up with a heavy heart, silent tears trailing down his cheeks. He could not blame the hawk for being a hawk, but his heart ached at seeing the baby kit ripped violently from his family. He could have shouted and frightened the hawk away, but the Medicine Man, Standing Bear, had taught him that all animals and plants exist in balance, each life depending on another's life to sustain it. Standing Bear had said that man has great power to upset that balance, and therefore has a great responsibility to not interfere with animal and plant life, except for food and other necessities. Running Wolf knew this to be true. He sustained his own life with the meat the hunters brought in, but the moments he spent with the animals had given him a tender heart. It pained him each time a life was ended, especially the life of a young one.

Running Wolf eased himself to the ground and stretched out on the grass, looking up at the small patch of blue sky. Why, he wondered, did the Great Spirit create a world of death, of disease, of pain? Why did the Great Spirit allow hunger and want, fear and hate? Why did the Great Spirit create boys with stick legs, and fathers who died at the hands of other men? Running Wolf knew of the Balance of Life, but he could not understand why there had to be the bad along with the good. The young man pondered on these questions as he drifted into a light sleep.

A distant rumble awakened Running Wolf, and he felt the ground beneath him trembling. He instinctively knew he was in danger. The thunder must have signaled a storm high on the mountain. The Sudden Great Waters were coming, and he was now trapped in the canyon! He jumped up and ran, limping toward the mouth of the canyon. A great wall of water came plummeting over the cliffs, filling the floor of the small canyon. Running Wolf felt himself swept up into the water. Branches from the beaver den surrounded him and struck his body. Twisting and tossing in the current of the churning water, he felt a sudden, searing pain in his arm as he was thrown violently against the rugged canyon wall. His face brushed against a small bush growing out of a crevice in the rock cliff, and he grabbed onto it with one hand, but soon the force of the Great Waters pulled him back down into the swirling mass of water and wood. Gasping for air, he could no longer keep his head above water and was sucked under, tumbling head over heels, pummeled by loose debris in the swirling water. He no longer knew which way was up. The pressure in his lungs became more and more intense. Finally, he attempted to take a breath, and his lungs filled with water.

Surprisingly, he felt himself being supported and lifted. He saw long, dark, flowing hair swirling around him and knew that the beautiful Spirit of the Water was carrying him. He looked up into her delicate face, and she smiled at him reassuringly. All the pain left him, and he felt exquisite peace as she carried him up, up, up until he emerged from the water. Once free of the churning cauldron below, the enchanting Spirit of the Water tenderly set Running Wolf on the sturdy back of a giant eagle, gliding just above the water. She kissed him and vanished back into her own world.

The powerful Spirit of the Wind lifted Running Wolf in wide ascending circles until they were out of the canyon. Running Wolf felt secure on the back of the magnificent eagle as they flew towards the Great Sun. He exhilarated in the freedom of flight as he felt the warm wind against his face and witnessed the earth moving swiftly beneath.

Closer and closer to the sun they flew, until Running Wolf found that they were flying over a land of sparkling light and beauty. The eagle circled downward and landed in a meadow adorned with brilliant flowers radiating a vast rainbow of colors that Running Wolf had never before seen. Running Wolf sensed that this was the end of his journey with the Wind, and he slipped off of the eagle's back. He was surprised at how easily he could move. He looked down at his legs. They were both perfect! He jumped and shouted for joy and ran around the meadow faster than he had ever imagined he could.

Running Wolf heard giggles and laughter behind him and quickly turned to look. A host of children were running behind him. They seemed happy to see him, and he let them catch up. They all ran and laughed together. At last he could run and play with other children, and so he ran and played until they all collapsed around each other, laughing amidst the tapestry of flowers. He sat still, surrounded by friends and beauty, watching the butterflies flutter and dance among the waves of colors.

"Where am I?" Running Wolf asked the children scattered around him.

"This is the Land of Eternal Light, where the Great Spirit dwells," answered an older girl child. Running Wolf looked at her and saw a radiant face of sweet and innocent beauty. Each of the children was surrounded by light that was coming from within them, or rather, as he began to see them more clearly, he realized that they *were* light. And then he saw his own light, the light that was him, radiating out from him.

"Am I dead?" he asked tentatively.

"Well, not really," answered the child. "The Great Spirit has permitted you to visit us. He wants us to teach you the answers to your questions. The Great Spirit is pleased with your kind and tender heart. He sees your heart is open and that it desires to learn. The time has now come for you to begin fulfilling your purpose on the earth."

Running Wolf became concerned. "I went to the canyon on my Manhood Quest to learn the purpose of my life. But the Sudden Great Waters came, and now I am here with you instead of in the canyon."

"Do not fear, Running Wolf," said the beautiful girl child. "All will be well. Tell us about your earth experience. You are so courageous to take on a mortal, imperfect body and live on the earth."

Running Wolf was surprised. "Don't you know what the earth is like? Mother Earth can be a dark and fearsome place. Why do you want to hear about that?"

The child laughed a sweet, crystal laugh that Running Wolf would never forget. "We know about the earth," she said, "but we don't really know what it is like because we have not yet experienced it. We are all looking forward to our own turn to go there and experience life."

Running Wolf looked at the beauty surrounding him, and felt the force of the incredible love of every child, every flower, every blade of grass. "Why would you want to leave a place like this and go to the earth where there is pain and sickness, hatred and fear, darkness and death?"

"For the same reason you did," answered the child with amusement, "to learn what perfect love is. We want to learn how to choose to love and how to choose to live in the Light."

"But you are all filled with love," exclaimed Running Wolf. "I can feel it. And you already live in the light."

"Yes, that is true," responded the girl child. "We live in light and love. We do it because that is all we know. We do not truly know what perfect light and perfect love are because we have known nothing else."

"I don't quite understand," said Running Wolf. "Why wouldn't you know what love and light are when you are surrounded by it?"

The child leaned over and cupped a vibrant blue flower with her hands. Blue light radiated outward, surrounding the flower and the child's hands. "What if the only color you ever saw was blue?" asked the child. "How would you really know what the color blue was if you never saw any other color to compare it to?

"Or what if all you ever ate was corn? How would you even know that you liked corn if you never tasted anything else to compare it to?

"Or what if you grew up in a village where there was only peace and plenty, where everyone was healthy and had abundant wealth. How would you ever know how blessed you were if you never saw poverty and hunger? What if you lived in a place where there was only poverty and hunger? How would you know that there was a better way to live if you never knew anything different? To truly know and experience something, we must experience the opposite."

"I am beginning to see," said Running Wolf. "The joy I felt on finding that my leg was whole was beyond description, because I know what it is like to not be able to run. But I still do not quite understand. What purpose is there in learning these lessons if it means leaving this place where you are already happy?"

The child came over and took Running Wolf's hand, placing it in hers. "You still have no remembrance of the Great Spirit, your Heavenly Father. Lay down among the flowers and close your eyes, and I will lift the veil of forgetfulness."

Running Wolf lay back in the emerald velvet grass and closed his eyes. The child squeezed his hand and watched him. Soon tears ran down the sides of his face. He opened his eyes and sat up.

"I do remember the Great Father. I see His brilliance. His brightness is beyond description. I feel the power of His love and how it fills me with unspeakable joy. I know of His infinite wisdom and knowledge. I deeply desire to be like Him. On the earth I wanted to be like the Medicine Man. He is the best man I know, and I wanted to learn what he knows and to act like he does. I now remember the same yearnings to learn what the Great Father knows and be like Him."

"That is correct, Running Wolf," said the girl child, still holding onto his hand. "That is why you chose to go to Mother Earth. The Great Father knows all. He knows the good and the evil, the light and the dark. With this knowledge He has true freedom of choice. In choosing only good, only love, and only light, He gains all power. We want to be like Him so we must also gain this knowledge."

"How do we gain it by going to Mother Earth?" asked Running Wolf.

"The only way we can truly know love is to experience the opposite," the beautiful child answered gently. "We cannot experience the opposite while we are in the presence of the Great Father because He chooses to have only perfection surrounding Him. He cannot have all power if He chooses anything different. He has therefore created Mother Earth as a place where we can experience the opposites, and He has given us a mortal body with weaknesses that allows us to learn by our own experience the good from the evil. As we experience the opposites of love, of good, of light and of life, we can truly have freedom of choice to choose what kind of being we really want to be. This choice gives us knowledge and power, and as we choose to love without condition, we become more like the Great Father. This is why we are so excited for you, and why we are looking forward to our own time on earth."

Running Wolf was excited. "Yes, yes! I see that this must be. I am grateful for what I learned from Mother Earth. But now I am glad to be finished with Mother Earth and to be here!" He started jumping and dancing for joy.

The children laughed and started dancing with him, but soon the girl of light and beauty stopped him and said, "You cannot stay here. You must return. The mission of your earth life is not complete."

"I do not want to return," protested Running Wolf. "I am happy here. I do not want to return to my heavy and lame body."

"Your body is your greatest teacher, Running Wolf," said the child. "You must be grateful for it."

"But why do I have to go back now that I am here?" asked Running Wolf.

"It is your choice whether you go back or not," said the child, "but your mission would be left incomplete, and that would have far-reaching consequences for you and for the people living on earth. Each person is given a mission to perform on Mother Earth. They may not be aware of it. Even if they are, they are often not aware of the effect this mission has on the entire world. Each person on earth is important to the Great Spirit, and each individual person can change the energy of the earth and what is happening on it."

"What is my mission?" queried Running Wolf.

"As you live your life and follow your heart," answered the child, "your mission will be complete. I can tell you only this much: part of your mission is to be a teacher. You will teach people the purpose of their life on Mother Earth so that they may find more light and joy in their hearts while they are experiencing the darkness that is necessary for their growth."

"Then I will return to Mother Earth," said Running Wolf.

The child pointed to the Great Eagle, and Running Wolf suddenly found himself again on the back of the Spirit of the Wind, circling down into the small canyon. The canyon was no longer peaceful and beautiful. Trees were uprooted. The swirling turbulent waters were gone, but the pool was twice its normal size with a stream of water flowing through the mouth of the canyon. The Great Eagle landed softly. Running Wolf saw a boy lying amidst the rubble of rocks, his forearm twisted in an unusual angle.

"Who is that poor boy?" asked Running Wolf.

"That is you, Running Wolf, " answered the Spirit of the Wind. "It is time for you to return."

Running Wolf shrank in dismay. "I cannot go back to that! Please take me back to the Land of Light!"

"It is important that you go, Running Wolf," replied the deep, soothing voice of the Great Eagle. "You still have more of life on our Mother Earth to experience, and you still have your mission to complete."

"I know that I must," whispered Running Wolf. "I choose to return."

Suddenly Running Wolf felt a pain in his arm so sharp that he cried out. He began coughing up water and pain ripped through his chest. He opened his eyes and found himself tangled among the rubble of rocks and branches left by the flood. The Great Eagle was nowhere to be seen. His body felt heavy and bruised. Every part of him seemed to ache, but the pain in his arm was worse than any pain he had known. He tried to sit up, but a knife-like piercing shot through his ribs, and as he started to move his arm, the pain was overwhelming. He lost all strength and fell back to the ground.

Tears again came to his eyes, and soon he was sobbing. He had been so happy in the Land of Light, so light and free. Earth life was too hard. He didn't know if he could make it. His heart ached with the loss of love that he had felt. He felt torn from his home of light, the place where he really belonged. He wondered why he had chosen to return.

Something scratched his leg, and he felt claws pricking his skin. He felt something climbing on him, but he was too over- whelmed with grief and pain to care. Then he felt fur on his face, and he discovered one of the small beaver kits whining and climb- ing all over him, sensing safety with this young man.

His sobs quieted. "Where is your family, Little Beaver? Were they all washed away?" Love for this tiny lost creature swelled in his heart and replaced a portion of the hollowness created by his grief. He immediately felt the need to protect and care for this young one.

Running Wolf considered his situation. His arm was broken, and probably some of his ribs. With water in his lungs he was at risk for the lung sickness. He knew he was all on his own. No one would come looking for him because he was on his Manhood Quest. It was time for him to truly be a man. He would have to fix his arm himself so he could return to the village right away. He lifted his head and surveyed his surroundings. Several feet away was a forked branch with one end lodged under a boulder. Nearby was a thick stick about a foot in length. He looked down at his leg. The yucca leaf had been washed away, but the fiber rope was still wrapped around his leg. He knew what he had to do.

The young man clenched his teeth and scooted over to the forked branch, each small movement filled with pain. He lifted his broken arm with his good arm, crying out from the pain, and placed his wrist in the fork. He pulled the yucca rope from off of his leg and wrapped it around his wrist, securing it to the branches. Bracing himself for the pain he knew would come, he started leaning backwards, pulling his arm straight. He screamed just as the forked branch came loose from the boulder. He fell backward, almost passing out.

As he lay there panting, he heard the sound of gentle laughter in the wind. All of a sudden he knew the children of light were watching and that he was being protected. He felt renewed strength and determination. He untied his wrist from the branches. His arm was much straighter now. It would have to do. He reached for the thick stick and tied it to his arm as tightly as he could, using his other hand. With his arm supported by the stick the pain was more tolerable. He then tested his legs, standing slowly. He was weak and wobbly, but he could walk. The beaver kit was whining at his feet. He took his buckskin shirt off and, using his teeth and his good hand, tied the sleeves around his ribs to support them. He then picked up the kit and put it inside his pouch. Immediately the kit settled down and was quiet.

Running Wolf looked around one last time at the small canyon, the place of his Vision of the Land of Light, and slowly turned towards home, his earth home. As he reached the opening of the canyon, he looked down over the green valley of his village. A faint smile crossed his lips. This life was indeed his choice, and although it meant hardship and pain, it also meant that he could come to know unconditional love, pure joy and heartfelt peace. He knew it would all be worth it. He started on his journey down the mountain to return to his valley home. Mother was waiting.

*   *   *

Grandmother stopped talking, but kept rocking in the ancient rocking chair in the parlor. "This was always my favorite story," she quietly reminisced. "Oma would tell this story with great animation, and with such a beautiful description of the Land of Eternal Light that I felt she had been there herself. She would never answer when I asked if she had, so I guess I won't find out until I am there myself."

"What an incredible story," said John. "Even though Oma made it up I would still like to believe that what Running Wolf learned in the Land of Light is true. It would make sense of all our questions."

"I have a question, Grandmother." Anne looked thoughtful.

"Certainly, my dear. What is it?" Grandmother stood up to pour Anne's bedtime herbal tea.

"Well," said Anne, "it's comforting to know that God gave me this body with weaknesses on purpose. It allows me to stop blaming myself and feeling guilty for all the stupid things I do."

"That's true, dear," interrupted Grandmother. "Our weaknesses, as part of our mortal existence, are given that we might learn. We don't have to blame ourselves for them, but it is important to be accountable for what we do with them. There are natural physical and spiritual consequences for all we do."

"That's my question," said Anne. "Even though I have a great desire to be a better person, I've made some mistakes which have had serious consequences. I don't know anyone who has completely and continually chosen love and light while on this earth. Maybe there are some people, but I don't know them. If we die before we learn to continually choose perfection, how can we return to this 'Land of Eternal Light' where God dwells, if only perfection exists there?"

"You told me you were a Christian, Anne," said Grandmother, as she gave Anne the tea. "Is that true?"

"Yes, Grandmother, we are Christians."

"I also believe in Jesus Christ," said Grandmother, sitting back down in the rocking chair. "Each person on this earth is given the choice to believe however they desire. Others may believe differently, but those of us who believe in Christ believe that His atonement makes up the difference for us. We believe that Christ willingly experienced all suffering and died so that each of us may be redeemed from our own mistakes and become perfect. If, in spite of our weaknesses, the desire of our hearts is to obey God and live in perfect love, and if we strive with all of our hearts to obtain this love, and if we have faith in the redeeming power of Jesus Christ, the grace of the atonement will perfect us and allow us to return to our Father again. That is why Jesus, the perfect Son of God, came to this earth."

Grandmother rocked quietly for a moment, and then continued. "The purpose of this earth is to learn and gain experience through our weaknesses and the weaknesses of others. This is how we experience 'the opposites' of life. Because our mortal bodies are imperfect, and we are surrounded by the darkness that exists on earth, God expects us to make mistakes as we learn. He provided for the atonement of Christ, which allows our weaknesses to become strengths through him, which in turn allows us to become perfect again."

"What did the child of light mean when she told Running Wolf that his body was his greatest teacher?" asked John.

"Obtaining physical bodies is another reason we are here on this earth. Many of the lessons we learn in life are learned because of the weaknesses, illnesses, pain, passions and emotions of our bodies. It is when our bodies are experiencing the greatest discomfort that we most earnestly seek for answers." Grandmother stood up to take Anne's teacup. "Our bodies can be our greatest teachers. The knowledge that our bodies are teaching us something with every illness and every pain allows us to better accept our difficulties. The lesson we learn may simply be to slow down and take better care of ourselves, or, on the other hand, it may bring a completely life-changing spiritual awareness that humbles us and brings us closer to God. Illness is a blessing. Pain is a blessing. I am grateful for all the pain and illness that I experienced in my life.

"Now, dear, it is time to rest. We don't want to get so carried away with stories that we forget what your wonderful body needs. You go back to bed, and I'll take John and put him to work doing a few more chores that I have a hard time doing by myself."

"Wait, Grandmother," protested Anne. "Isn't there a Dream Picture that goes with this story? I'll sleep much better if I can listen to the Dream Picture."

"Oh, all right. John, will you follow us into the bedroom and turn on the music? Then make yourself comfortable at the end of Anne's bed. I have changed this Dream Picture a bit from the way Oma used to tell it. I have made it a little more relevant to modern times, and this seems to work better for people dependent on technology."

* * *

Make yourself comfortable and listen to Dream Picture 5 on Track 2 of CD 2.

Chapter 6

THE SECRET OF GRATITUDE

Sunlight poured through the lace-curtained windows. Anne opened her eyes and followed her childlike impulse to rush to the window and see what wonders the outside world held. As she gazed on the vast brightness of white surrounding the little house, she stretched, taking in a deep breath. This was great. She could take a deep breath, and the breath didn't cause her to cough. She smiled, and leaning on the window-ledge, viewed the beauty of the sun-drenched landscape. White icing dripped from tree branches, marshmallows capped each fence post, and the ice-covered pond reflected the azure sky. Anne stayed by the window, absorbing the sun and the beauty.

Anne pondered the things that Grandmother had talked about the day before. She had always believed she was ill because she had done something wrong, and that God was punishing her. But Grandmother had described illness as a blessing from God. That thought was almost more than Anne could comprehend. And yet Grandmother's words resonated in Anne's heart, as if she had heard them before.

Anne saw a Bible on the nightstand. She picked it up and sat in the rocking chair near the bed. She searched for a verse in First Thessalonians she had heard her minister preach about. It took her a moment to find it in the fifth chapter:

"In every thing give thanks: for this is the will of God in Christ Jesus concerning you."

Anne had always thanked God for her blessings and had frequently prayed for help with her problems. But she could see now that she had never considered thanking God for her problems. If what Grandmother had said was true, that each of her problems was a blessing that allowed her to learn, then she should be giving thanks 'in every thing,' as the scriptures said.

85

Both the good things and the bad things are a part of life, and they all have purpose, even though she didn't always know what it was. Anne slowly slipped from the rocking chair and knelt by the bed. "Dear God, I don't know why I have to be sick. I don't know why I hurt all the time. I don't know why I am so weak that I have a hard time properly caring for my family. But now I am beginning to understand that there is purpose to everything that happens to me. The scriptures say that these things are Your will for me. I am beginning to see that these difficult experiences are for my good, even though I may never know the reason, at least in this life.

"Heavenly Father, I wish to obey You, and so now I give thanks in all things, the experiences that seem bad to me, along with the good experiences. I am thankful for the pain... No. I can't do it. I'm not thankful for the pain. That is more than I can be right now."

She stood slowly and began to get dressed. The appearance of the sun meant that she and John would be leaving today.

As Anne finished dressing, Grandmother knocked on the bedroom door and opened it slightly. "Would you like some breakfast, dear? June just called and said that the tow-truck pulled your car from that nasty ditch. John and George went to get it, and June said it would be about an hour before they returned."

Anne nodded and followed Grandmother into the kitchen. The table was set with two bowls of steaming oatmeal covered with nuts, seeds and apple slices and colorful mugs of herbal tea with floating orange and lemon slices. After a simple blessing on the food given by Anne, they ate in contented silence.

Anne rose to help Grandmother clear the table. "You sit and rest, dear. I'll have this clean in no time. We want you well rested for your trip."

Anne sat back down. "I feel so much better. I'm not sure I want to go to another doctor and tell my story again and have them poke and prod. You've taught me what I need to know."

"You have learned about healing from your heart, Anne, and that will make all the difference. But I've heard about this clinic you're going to, and they'll also teach you the best way to care for your body while you are healing. You can't separate your body from your mind and your spirit. You must take good care of it as well."

"I trust your opinion, Grandmother." Anne leaned her elbows

on the table and placed her chin in her hands. She noticed the sun-light streaming between the lemon-yellow curtains. "Look at the dust dancing in the sunbeam! I haven't watched a sunbeam since I was a little girl." Her eyes sparkled as they followed the dancing sunbeam with delight. "It is so peaceful here Grandmother. I almost wish I didn't have to go home."

"It wasn't so peaceful here when I had a pack of children running around," chuckled Grandmother. "Remember, to every thing there is a time and a season. Your season of quiet will come in due time."

"Yes, I am grateful for my 'pack of children,'" smiled Anne, "even Rachel, my youngest. Or it would be better to say 'especial-ly Rachel,' because she is my greatest challenge and is teaching me my greatest lessons."

"I am glad to hear you say that, dear," said Grandmother, fold-ing the dishtowel and hanging it over the oven handle. "Sowing gratitude reaps rich rewards. If we can truly feel grateful for every-thing, the difficult things as well as those that are easy, the illness as well as the health, the weakness as well as the strength, the dark as well as the light, our lives become abundant indeed.

"That all sounds good, Grandmother, but it's not that easy. I just can't be grateful for my pain. It has ruined my life."

"I have another story that might help you," said Grandmother. "Would you like to hear it?"

"You know I would, Grandmother," said Anne. "When you tell your stories I feel like I am inside of them, watching Running Wolf with my own two eyes. I could listen to you all day."

"Then come into the parlor and we'll meet Running Wolf one last time."

* * *

Chief Coyote Eyes watched warily as the two pale men with hairy faces approached, making signs of peace. The war-riors were gathered around him, weapons ready. He motioned for them to keep their weapons down for the moment. The hairy faces were leading three large animals the Chief had never seen before, although he thought he knew what they were. Neighboring tribes had talked about these pale-face men from across the Great

Waters that called themselves 'Spaniards.' They could ride these large animals they called 'horses.' Chief Coyote Eyes was curious about these strange men. The Others said these men traded unusual and new things for the villagers' necklaces and bracelets. There had been no malice, nothing that should cause the Chief to be concerned. However, as the men came closer, he felt a sense of uneasiness. "Tell Running Wolf to come," he told Crooked Feather. "I have need of his discerning wisdom."

The Spaniards entered the village. With language signs and a few words of The People, they indicated they came in peace to trade. Running Wolf, now tall, slender, and muscular, limped up to Chief Coyote Eyes just as the men with hairy faces expressed their interest in the beautiful silver jewelry of The People.

"Keep the villagers from getting too close to these men," said Running Wolf quietly to the Chief. "My heart does not feel quite right about them."

"I agree, Running Wolf. They seem to be harmless, and I want to see what they have, but we will be wary." The Chief motioned for the chattering and excited villagers to stay a respectful distance from the men.

Running Wolf also felt a great wonder about these men and their possessions, but the responsibility he felt to the villagers was greater. The ceremony that gave him the title of Medicine Man was only a moon earlier, and Running Wolf worried that he lacked the experience and wisdom to deal with the unusual strangers. He was young, only twenty-four summers, and he had been surprised when the dying Standing Bear told the village elders that Running Wolf was ready to take his place. He missed his old friend's wise words of advice and encouragement.

The men lifted a large load off the back of one of the horses. They laid the load on the ground and opened it. Everyone inched closer to see what the men had. They first picked up a large pot and indicated that it was for cooking. They banged on it to show that it was made of metal, and threw it hard on the ground, demonstrating that it would not break. They set it near the villagers, and a few women came closer to inspect it.

The men with hairy faces then brought out several bolts of linen and wool cloth. The villagers had never seen woven cloth before. The fabric was dyed in brilliant and appealing colors. One of the men wrapped a cloth around himself to show how the fabric draped around the body. The women giggled at the sight, but came close as the men laid the bolts of fabric down.

They then pulled out strings of colorful beads. The men said they were made from 'porcelain' and 'glass.' The villagers exclaimed at the brightness and variety of colors of the beads. They had several different colors of stones for their necklaces, and silver was easily found, but they had never seen such beautiful colors as those found in the porcelain beads. They were further enticed by the sparkling nature of the cut glass. The Spaniards laid the beads on a cloth close to the villagers, and many crowded around to touch and examine the wonder of the beads.

Again, the pale men opened a cloth and revealed what appeared to be knives, very different from the flint and obsidian knives of The People. The wooden handles were intricately carved, and the blades were made of metal. One of the pale-faces picked up a stick and started whittling, showing how sharp the knife was. An older brave, Crazy Hawk stood up from looking at the beads and put his hand out for the knife. He felt the edge of the blade with his thumb and was surprised when he drew a little blood. The warriors became excited and circled around, picking up the knives and cutting branches, leather, and anything else they could find.

The Spaniards indicated they wanted to trade these things for the jewelry of the villagers. The Chief was incredulous. Stones and silver were plentiful, and the adornments were not held to be of unusual worth among The People. Yet, that was all that these strange men asked for. Crazy Hawk took off his necklace and encouraged his family to also bring their jewelry.

"Wait, Crazy Hawk!" said the Chief. "We must discuss what is happening so that we can make sure that trading with these men is best for the people of the village."

"What is there to discuss?" asked Crazy Hawk impatiently. "The Others in the Great Valley were pleased with their trading, and no harm came to them. Look at all these beautiful things. That red cloth would look beautiful on my daughter, Red Dawn. Surely this is a good thing."

"I feel uneasy about this," said Running Wolf. "Something is not quite right here. Why would these men want only that which is of little worth to us?"

"Because they are stupid," answered Spotted Owl. "Look at those hairy faces. They must be stupid. If we can make a good trade with them, we should do it." The villagers all voiced approval for the words of Spotted Owl and gathered around the men to trade.

Running Wolf stood back and watched the villagers. He felt their excitement as they obtained their new belongings. Maybe he was being too cautious because he was so new with this responsibility. Running Wolf said no more. He smiled at the villagers as they showed him their treasures, and was excited when his mother, Dancing Water, showed him the sky-blue fabric and the beads she had received in exchange for her necklace and bracelet. She also showed him a thin, sharp sliver of metal called a 'needle,' and a long fine string she called 'thread.' She told him that the man who gave them to her had showed her how they were used to sew the cloth together. She hurried to put her new treasures in their lodge.

Old Crazy Hawk invited the Spaniards to eat with him and sleep in his lodge that night. Chief Coyote Eyes assigned several braves to guard the lodge and keep an eye on the men, but the night was calm and quiet.

Running Wolf was up before dawn the following morning, watching the lodge of Crazy Hawk and pondering over the nature of these strange men. He wondered why they were here in the land of The People. He had mixed feelings about these men, as if they were both a curse and a blessing to the villagers. As the sun peered over the mountain, the men emerged from the lodge of Crazy Hawk, yawning and stretching in the early morning light. Running Wolf noticed that one of the men was coughing, and that he seemed to have a rash on his pale skin. He could see that this man was sick, but the Spaniards seemed anxious to leave, and he was glad to stand with the other villagers and watch the wonder of the pale men riding horses down the mountain valley. He hoped that they would not return again.

"One pale-face seemed sick," said Running Wolf to Crazy Hawk.

"Yes," said Crazy Hawk, "he was coughing a lot during the evening meal. We gave him some tea for the lungs, but he continued to cough through the night. This morning it looked like he had nettle rash all over him. We offered to bring you to see him, but they seemed anxious to leave."

"What did the pale men talk about?" the Chief asked Crazy Hawk.

"They asked where we got our silver. I told them there were caves all over these mountains where silver was plentiful. I told them where several of the caves were, and they gave me this." Crazy Hawk showed them a long, tube-like instrument made from a yellow metal, with clear smooth stones, like the cut beads, on the ends. The Chief looked into the narrow end and jumped back. Carefully, he looked again. "What is far away becomes close," he said.

"This will make hunting much easier," exclaimed Crazy Hawk. "We are blessed that these men came to the village."

"Yes we are," said Running Wolf. "Something was not quite right about their visit, but our village is blessed. We should give thanks to the Great Spirit."

Twelve suns had passed since the visit of the Spaniards. Dancing Water was busy sewing on the blue cloth. She wanted to surprise Running Wolf. He believed that she was making a dress for herself, but she was actually making a shirt for him. He would look so handsome in this shirt that was bluer than the morning sky. "He will truly look like the wise Medicine Man that he is," she thought proudly.

Singing Bird ran through the door of the lodge and stopped breathlessly. "Do you know where Running Wolf is? My mother has need of him."

"He is working with Crooked Feather, helping him repair his canoe. What need does White Feather have of my son?"

"Red Dawn, the youngest daughter of Crazy Hawk, is very ill. Mother has been caring for her all night, but feels she is getting worse."

Dancing Water quickly put down the blue cloth "When you find him tell him I'll meet him at the lodge of Crazy Hawk with his healing pouches."

Singing Bird ran back out the door to find Running Wolf while Dancing Water gathered her son's supplies.

Running Wolf entered the lodge and went directly to the gasping child. She seemed to be about eleven or twelve summers in age. It was with great effort that Red Dawn drew each breath, and he feared that death was near. He noticed a fine red rash all over her skin. Running Wolf was dismayed. "This looks like the same sickness that the Spaniard had. How long has she been sick?"

Crazy Hawk looked with questioning towards his weeping wife, White Crane. She wiped at her tears and told Running Wolf, "She has been coughing and warm for a couple of days, but didn't have difficulty breathing until last night. That was when the rash appeared."

"It must be a sickness that jumps from one person to another. Is anyone else sick?"

White Crane looked frightened. "I have begun coughing," she said.

"We must keep everyone that has been close to Red Dawn in this lodge," said Running Wolf. "This must not spread through the village. Who has Red Dawn been spending time with?"

"She spends a lot of time caring for the little children of her brother and sister, who are both married," replied White Crane, "but this last week she has been gathering nuts in the forest with her best friend, Falling Waters, and has spent only a few hours with the little ones."

"Where have you spent your time this last week?" queried Running Wolf of White Crane.

"I have been here sewing a dress for Red Dawn out of the red cloth the Spaniards brought."

"Crazy Hawk, did anyone else eat or sleep with you the night the Spaniards were here?" questioned Running Wolf.

"My son and our friend Spotted Owl came and ate with us, my son's wife helped serve us, and my grandchildren ran in and out, but no one else spent the night here except my wife and Red Dawn," answered Crazy Hawk.

"Mother," said Running Wolf, "go to the lodges of the son and daughter of Crazy Hawk and tell them to stay with their families in their homes. Tell them not to allow anyone in their lodges that is not in this room right now. Then fetch Spotted Owl and Falling Waters and bring them here. Afterwards I would like you to go bathe in the stream and wash any spirit of sickness away that may have attached itself to you from this short moment here. I must stay here and will need you free to carry messages for me to the Chief and the other villagers."

Dancing Water left to carry out the bidding of Running Wolf while he opened his pouch and sprinkled corn pollen over the weakening Red Dawn. The Medicine Man started chanting quietly as he prepared the healing potions.

Red Dawn was dead. The grieving White Crane started the death cry, a high, mournful warbling. Falling Waters joined in. Soon Running Wolf heard others outside the door of the lodge crying the melancholy wail. The village knew he had failed. He had spent the entire night entreating the Great Spirit with his chants and working with White Feather, the medicine woman, in treating Red Dawn with herbs and poultices. But she had simply become weaker and had cried restlessly with the burning of the rash. Her mother rinsed her with cool water, the only thing that seemed to bring comfort. Then as the sky turned red with the approach of the sun, the dawn accepted the spirit of its namesake, and she was gone.

Running Wolf knew he had done the best that he could, but he still grieved over the loss of this sweet child and wished he could have done better. He knew that the trouble was not yet over. Crazy Hawk was beginning to chill and complain of a sore throat, and his wife was weakening with fever. As he examined them, they both had strange white spots in their mouths of a type that Running Wolf had never seen before. He was certain that this sickness belonged to the pale men, not to The People. He did not know how to make it leave.

Running Wolf and White Feather discussed everything they knew about fevers, sore throats, lung sickness and rashes. They decided to use all the remedies they were aware of to keep this disease from spreading through the village. White Feather left to gather some of the plants that they did not already have, while Running Wolf prepared the plants that he had with him to give to Crazy Hawk and his wife. He ceremoniously chanted during their preparation, entreating the Great Spirit to put His healing spirit into the herbs.

Red Dawn's friend, Falling Waters, watched as Running Wolf prepared his potions. "Is there anything I can do to assist you, Running Wolf?" she asked.

Running Wolf turned to look at Falling Waters. He had been busy all night with Red Dawn and had not paid her much attention. She smiled shyly, and asked again, "Is there anything I can do for you?"

There was something very familiar about this child who was approaching womanhood. He had not really been aware of her the last year as he had been learning from the ailing Standing Bear. He saw now that Falling Waters would soon become a delicate woman, and, as she smiled, he knew there was something about her that was hidden away in his memory.

"Here, Falling Waters, take this bowl of leaves and crush them with this stick. That's right. You're doing a great job." Running Wolf saw that she seemed to know what she was doing.

"I have been learning from White Feather," she stated simply.

"How old are you now, Falling Waters?" asked Running Wolf.

"I am just finishing my thirteenth summer. I was born the day you returned from your Manhood Quest, the day that the new waterfall appeared on the mountain" answered Falling Waters. "My mother thought that my birth was on a momentous day because of the message your Vision brought to the Village. I was brought up on the lessons that your Vision taught us, and I have always watched you and wanted to be like you. That is why I am learning from White Feather."

Running Wolf was touched by Falling Water's humble admiration. He was pleased that the stories of his vision were being taught to the children. He continued to watch Falling Waters out of the corner of his eye and gave her more work to do. She learned quickly and followed his instructions with precision.

Running Wolf soon became absorbed in caring for Crazy Hawk and his wife. Spotted Owl also started getting a fever and complained of painful eyes. By evening the married son of Crazy Hawk started showing symptoms of the sickness, and was brought over to the lodge to be cared for. Running Wolf realized that anyone that had come in close contact with the sick Spaniard was getting the illness. He was hoping that it was only close contacts that would become sick.

Two of the grandchildren of Crazy Hawk started getting sick and were brought into the lodge. Running Wolf and White Feather used every skill and treatment they had. Many of the plants they used seemed to ease the burning of the skin, or lighten the tightness of the lungs, but after two days White Crane, the wife of Crazy Hawk, crossed to the land of spirits, and several hours later one of the grandchildren died as well. Running Wolf's gentle heart was grieving. The villagers were beginning to panic and complain that the Great Spirit was punishing them for letting the hairy men into their village.

Discouraged, Running Wolf slipped out of the lodge in the middle of the night and found himself wandering into the forest, headed for his old "Watching Place." He came to the clear spring, stripped off his clothes and washed himself with the cool, refreshing water. As he put his clothes back on he felt renewed. He sat down next to the old willow bush, now overgrown, and waited and watched. Soon he saw a shadow appear and knew it had come out of the den, built on the edge of the stream. His old friend Beaver had come to say hello to him. Beaver nuzzled up under the hand of Running Wolf, anxious to feel the loving strokes that he always received. Running Wolf scratched Beaver's head, and then Beaver turned over to have his tummy scratched. Running Wolf couldn't help but laugh. He rolled on the grass, tussling with Beaver as he had so many years ago when Beaver was just a little ball of fluff.

After a period of play, Running Wolf lay in the lush grass of the little clearing while Beaver went to nibble on a nearby willow. He looked up at the full moon and remembered how he had found Beaver, or rather how Beaver had found him, broken on the rocks in that small canyon up on the mountain. He played through his mind the Vision of the Land of Light once more. He realized that the words of Falling Waters had brought him here to remember. He began to feel the peace of that land, and he remembered the words of the beautiful Child of Light. He remembered the laugh of the beautiful girl-child. He would never forget her sweet, crystal laugh.

Running Wolf remembered the day the Spaniards arrived in the village. Because of the Vision, he knew that this experience must be something that the Great Spirit had planned for the village. He remembered the unusual mixture of caution and blessing that he had felt when they came. He remembered the strong feeling that he should express gratitude for the blessings that these strange men had given to the village. Now, with several deaths and more illness appearing, Running Wolf had a harder time feeling the desire to express gratitude, but he also knew that there must be a purpose to this grievous experience.

Running Wolf had learned long ago that true gratitude for all things brought great abundance into his life, and many times the difficult things he was experiencing improved or resolved when he expressed appreciation for them to the Great Spirit. He stood up in the light of the full moon and stretched his arms upward.

"Oh, Great Spirit, the Great Father of all, I know not why these men from across the Great Waters came to our village, bringing evil spirits of sickness. I do not know why the family of Crazy Hawk, and especially the children, must die. My heart aches and is beginning to break with grief over them. Even though I know they are now finding joy in the Land of Eternal Light, each one of them takes a part of my heart with them. I do not know the reasons for these things, but Great Father, I know that there are reasons, and I thank you for them. I thank you for this sickness that is spreading through the village. I thank you for the fears of the villagers. I thank you for the death of Red Dawn, and her mother, and the little one that joined you just this afternoon. Please allow me to inspire the villagers to let go of their fears and to also feel gratitude."

Running Wolf followed his plea with alternating chants to the Great Father and stillness to listen for answers. Finally, as the sky turned from navy to a deep royal blue, he felt peace in his heart. He knew what he should do. He spent some time gathering plants and then said goodbye to Beaver as he headed back to his own lodge. The sun was ready to spill over the mountain as he asked his mother, from her doorway, to gather the villagers together in front of the lodge of Crazy Hawk. He did not want to get too close to her in case the sickness was already growing within him. Then he headed back to the lodge that was now filled with grief and death.

When he returned, Crazy Hawk was out of bed and caring for his second grandson, Gray Wolf. This beloved child was crying from the burning of the rash and the pain in his eyes. Crazy Hawk looked up at Running Wolf, his face gaunt and full of anguish. "I'm glad you're back, Running Wolf. I am feeling a little better and my rash has lessened, but little Gray Wolf here is getting worse by the moment. And they brought over Yellow Lily, my sweet grand-daughter, who is running a high fever and seems to have lost her hearing. I am so frightened, Running Wolf. I should have listened to your caution about the hairy men. I wish I had never brought them into my lodge with their evil spirits of sickness. This sickness is because of my foolishness. I have brought death and ruin to my family and to the village. Here is the sharp knife I received from these men. Cut my face. Cut my arms and my chest. I must be pun-ished, Running Wolf."

"What we must do, Crazy Hawk," responded Running Wolf gently, "is to give gratitude to the Great Spirit, not punish you."

"What do we have to thank the Great Spirit for?" Crazy Hawk cried. "The wife of my bosom has been torn from my arms, along with the daughter of my old age and my littlest grandson. More are getting sick. My heart is broken. Certainly the Great Spirit is already punishing me. Maybe if you punish me, the Great Spirit won't need to, and the rest of my family will be saved."

"Crazy Hawk." Running Wolf sat down next to the distraught man. "This sickness has nothing to do with punishment. One of the Spaniards had the sickness, and everyone that was close to him for a time is also getting the sickness. Spotted Owl is not of your fam-ily, and he is also getting sick."

"Yes, but he also encouraged the villagers to accept the pale men," said Crazy Hawk, standing weakly, brandishing the knife. "He also is being punished. Please take my knife and mark me, or I will do it myself."

Running Wolf jumped up and easily wrestled the knife from the ill old man. Crazy Hawk sank to the ground, heartbroken and humiliated. Running Wolf squatted next to him, placing his hand gently on the arm of the old brave. "Please listen to me, Crazy Hawk. My heart also is in great pain. I am a new Medicine Man, and I am failing to keep these people we all love alive. I have been blaming myself for being a Medicine Man without power. I lack the wisdom and experience of Standing Bear. I have been in anguish at my failures. But I just spent the night entreating the

Great Spirit for the answers to all that I cannot do myself. The feeling has been very strong in my heart this morning that there is a purpose in all of this. I do not know why we must go through this anguish. I do not know the purpose of the sickness and death in your lodge and in our village, but I know there is one.

"Listen, the villagers are gathering. Sit near me by the door, and hear what I have to say. Then we can talk again, if you desire."

Crazy Hawk meekly pulled himself over next to the door and leaned against the inside wall. Running Wolf pulled back the buffalo blanket covering the entrance and stood facing his friends. Most of their faces were filled with fear, and several were taut with anger. Running Wolf closed his eyes and silently entreated the strength of the Great Spirit to be upon him and upon his people, that they all would find healing, a healing of the heart as well as of the body.

"My friends," began the new Medicine Man, with a strength of voice that he did not feel within, "we are faced with a disaster greater than our village has faced in many generations. The Spaniards who brought such beautiful things to our village also brought a sickness that does not listen to my chants. So far only those who were close to the sick pale man have come down with the sickness, but our friends in this lodge who lay sick and dying have been among you before they became ill. There is a possibility that some of you may also get the sickness."

A murmur rose among the people, and several of the women started weeping. One man cried out, "I think we need another Medicine Man. We should go to the Others and bring back a Medicine Man with more experience and power."

"That may be true," answered Running Wolf, "but please listen to me first. It is time for us to have a feast and a ceremony. It is time for us to acknowledge how we are indebted to the Great Spirit for all that we are and all that we have. We have been living in peace and prosperity for so long that we have been negligent in expressing appreciation to Mother Earth for her rich soil that produces much food, to the Sun for warmth and light, to the Rain for our abundance of water, to the animals for giving their lives so that we may be fed, and especially to the Great Father for our health and the abundant lives we have been living."

"This is no time for a feast," someone yelled. "People are dying."

"That is especially why we need a feast and the Ceremony of Thanksgiving," said Running Wolf. "As we give gratitude and praise to the Great Father for every thing, even for the Spaniards and the sickness and the deaths, the bad spirits surrounding the village will have to leave. They come when there is fear, and while they stay here the sickness will continue. We must thank the Great Father for all that is good as well as all that seems bad at this time. We must trust that all we are experiencing in this village will be for our best good. If we fill our hearts with love and gratitude and praise, our fear will be replaced, and the bad spirits that are keeping the sickness here will have to leave, because they cannot live where fear is not."

Chief Coyote Eyes stepped forward. "I agree with Running Wolf. He is of the same heart and speaking the same words as would Standing Bear, who always served our village well. We must change our hearts to rid our lodges and our village of the bad spirits so that the sickness may stop. Everyone go to your lodges and prepare for the feast tonight, as Running Wolf prepares for the Ceremony of Thanksgiving. Change your words of fear to words of gratitude and praise. These are my words."

Murmuring continued, but the villagers dispersed, and Running Wolf breathed a sigh of relief as he went back into the lodge. "White Feather, I know you are tired from all your work over the last few days, but could you do without me today while I gather what is needed and prepare myself for the ceremony?"

White Feather smiled at Running Wolf. "What you have to do is more important at this time. All our combined knowledge has not helped these people. Prepare yourself. Falling Waters knows much and is a good apprentice. She will assist me while you are gone."

As the villagers were finishing their feast, the Medicine Man emerged from his lodge, purified after the cleansing rites, and stood with painted face and ceremonial dress. A necklace of combined bear and wolf claws adorned his bare, muscled and oiled chest, and the headdress of eagle feathers, presented to him by Standing Bear, allowed him to appear larger and full of power. The drums were answering each heartbeat as the villagers watched him in awe. Not one pair of eyes noticed the limping gait of the shriveled leg. No one had ever before seen the true magnificence of Running Wolf, the Medicine Man.

Running Wolf slowly entered the open circle surrounding the fire, dancing to the rhythm of the drums and the song of the chanters. The ceremonial dances were the hardest part of being a Medicine Man, at least for Running Wolf. He had spent hours with Standing Bear, learning how to use his lame leg so that he could do the dances correctly. Now that he was in the midst of the drums, however, he felt transformed into another realm and was floating through the steps, expressing through song and movement the Ceremony of Gratitude. New parts of the dance came to him, movements that symbolized illness and death. The beating drums and chanting songs began to draw the villagers into the trance-like dancing of the Medicine Man, and soon other braves joined in, expressing through dance the gratitude of their hearts. When it was time, all the villagers danced, allowing their bodies to open up the feelings of their hearts to the Great Spirit. The darkness of the night enveloped them as they danced on.

Running Wolf woke with a start. He opened his eyes, and found Falling Waters kneeling in front of him.

"I wanted to give time for your spirit to return from its night wanderings, so I just touched you gently," she whispered. "I did not mean to startle you. I am sorry."

Running Wolf saw the light of dawn shining through the door of the lodge behind Falling Waters. He remembered that after putting away his ceremonial dress he had returned to the lodge of Crazy Hawk to watch over the little ones. "My spirit has returned. Thank you for waking me, Falling Waters. I did not intend to fall asleep."

"It is good for you to sleep," protested Falling Waters. "We desire that you have a clear mind to guide us through these difficult days. You have not received enough sleep while this sickness has been upon us. I would not bother you now except that I had a dream that I feel is important for you to know."

"What is your dream, child?" asked Running Wolf.

"I have been watching how Crazy Hawk, his son and Spotted Owl have begun to get better from this illness, and everyone else with the sickness has died or are dying. I wondered about this. What would cause the evil spirits of the sickness to leave the very men that kept the Spaniards in our village? Why are they the ones spared from death? These questions were going through my mind while you were at the Ceremony of Gratitude. Then, when I fell asleep, I had this dream. In the dream, I saw Crazy Hawk, Spotted Owl, and the son of Crazy Hawk eating with the Spaniards. I knew that this dream was the answer to my questions, but when I woke, I could not see how it held the answer. That is why I have come to you. I have need of your wisdom."

"All that you saw in the dream was the men eating?" asked Running Wolf. "You did not see any medicine that the sick pale man may have used? You did not hear them speak concerning the illness?"

"No, Running Wolf," Falling Waters answered despondently. "I saw nothing else, and I heard not their words."

Running Wolf stood up and started pacing. He, too, could feel the importance of this dream. It was too simple. It could not hold the answers. But he felt the truth of the words of Falling Waters. Her dream held the answers to ridding his village of the spirits of this sickness.

"What were the men eating, Falling Waters? Could you see what they were eating?"

"I could not see what they were eating. I should have looked in my dream at what they were eating." Falling Waters hung her head.

"We were eating the liver of a dog." Crazy Hawk sat up. "Ever since our days of hunger, when we had to eat our dogs to survive the winters, that has been my favorite food. We killed a dog for the feast with the Spaniards, and my wife fed us the liver. Then, when we got sick, my daughter brought us another liver of a dog. She thought that it would cheer me up. I have been sharing it with my son and Spotted Owl, but the women and children do not care for it and would not take it."

"The liver of a dog! Could that be the answer? Is there something in the spirit of the liver of the dog that is more powerful than the spirit of the sickness of the pale men?"

Soon Running Wolf was sending messages to the villagers. The People had lived with abundant food for many years, and many dogs had grown old rather than being used for food as they had in the past. It was time, once again, for the dogs to serve The People. The dogs were killed ceremoniously, with chants of gratitude to the spirit of each dog for giving its life to allow the Sickness to be stayed. By evening every person in the village was eating the liver of a dog.

Over the next few days, Gray Wolf and Yellow Lily, the grandchildren of Crazy Hawk, died. They had been so weak they could not eat. The sickness fell on others, including Falling Waters, White Feather and Running Wolf himself, but they were all fed more liver, and the severe lung sickness stayed away. From that time on, the spirit of the sickness became weak, and did not overtake the lives of The People.

Running Wolf emerged from the lodge of Crazy Hawk. It had been over a moon since Red Dawn had first become sick and Running Wolf had entered into this lodge of devastation. He had not known that this place would be both his home and his trial of fire for such a long time. He strength was finally returning, and no sickness had appeared in ten suns. He knew the crisis was over. He was ready to go home, where Dancing Water was waiting with his new blue shirt.

"May I assist you with your pouch, Running Wolf? You have much to carry." Falling Waters appeared at his side, dressed in a new doeskin dress, decorated with beads from the Spaniards. She had never been very ill and had gone back to her own lodge two days earlier.

"Yes, Falling Waters. I would be pleased to have you carry my pouch. You served both me and The People well, and I trust you with it." Running Wolf felt great affection for this beautiful childwoman. He had come to depend on her skills when he lay sick with fever. He remembered her gentle, cool touch on his hot brow. He was comfortable having her at his side.

"Running Wolf! Have you heard the news?" Crooked Feather came running towards Running Wolf and Falling Waters, breathing hard.

"Tell me, Crooked Feather, what have you heard?" said Running Wolf.

"I was down in the valley hunting and met Swift Antelope, one of the Others. He was alone, without food or weapon. The Spaniards had returned to the village of the Others in the Great Valley with many warriors on horses. They were all captured by these hairy pale men and taken away. Swift Antelope escaped, the only one from his village who got away. Burned and empty lodges in other nearby villages showed that they had also been taken prisoners."

Crooked Feather grabbed the arm of Running Wolf in his large hand. "Listen to this. Swift Antelope met a woman from the Village of the Meadow who had also escaped from the Spaniards. She told him that all of her people were slaves, digging for silver in the caves. All the other villages knew of the sickness in our village. The Spaniards were angry with the sick pale man because he left the sickness with us and they could not use our villagers for slaves. They did not come to capture us because of the sickness and thought we would all die."

Crooked Feather grabbed the other arm of Running Wolf and looked him in the eye. "I thought you were crazy, Running Wolf, when you performed the Ceremony of Gratitude while people were dying. But you were right about being grateful for the sickness. The sickness saved our village.

"I told Swift Antelope we did have sickness in our village, and that many had died from it, but that the evil spirits were now leaving. He said that if the sickness was leaving, that we should leave as well, so that the Spaniards could not find us and make us slaves. I brought Swift Antelope back with me, and we just finished talking with the Chief. He wants you to come to his lodge with the other elders of the council."

Running Wolf turned back to the door where Crazy Hawk was standing. "Crazy Hawk, did you hear that?"

"Yes, Running Wolf," Crazy Hawk cried. "This is terrible! We just have been released from the evil spirits of the sickness, and now we must leave our homes."

"No, Crazy Hawk, this is not terrible," said Running Wolf. "Don't you see what has happened? The sickness you brought into the village has *saved* the village." Running Wolf went over to

Crazy Hawk and knelt in front of him. "I honor you, Crazy Hawk. You have sacrificed your family to save the village. My heart is filled with gratitude and honor to you and the spirits of your family who gave their lives to save the rest of us. May the Great Spirit fill your heart with peace."

Running Wolf stood to follow Crooked Feather to the lodge of Chief Coyote Eyes. He suddenly heard laughter from behind him—a clear, crystal laugh that he remembered from long ago. He turned to look for the exquisite Child of Light, and smiled at finding Falling Waters, who was laughing with joy for the salvation of the village.

* * *

G randmother!" exclaimed Anne. "You mean Falling Waters was…"

"Oma never said more than that," interrupted Grandmother. "She would just smile and let us decide for ourselves who Falling Waters was."

Anne sat pensively, considering the story Grandmother had told. "Dog liver. Ugh. Why did Oma have the villagers eat dog liver for their medicine?"

"I asked Oma the same thing when I was little," laughed Grandmother. "I couldn't think of anything worse to eat than dog liver. Oma told me that they had eaten dog when she had lived with the Indians during that harsh winter. Her Indian friend told how her people had become infected with measles from white children. Because the Indians had never had measles before, they had no inherent immunity. What was usually a simple childhood disease to the white men was deadly to the Indians, and many in their tribe were dying. Somehow they discovered that the measles was much less severe when they ate dog liver, and that discovery saved the tribe. That's why Oma used it in her story, but she didn't know why the dog liver would make a difference. But I think I know why.

"I recently learned that dog liver is extremely high in Vitamin A; so high, in fact, that if too much is eaten, it can be toxic. It has been discovered that high levels of Vitamin A will stop the measles virus, and the doctors in third world countries are now using these high doses of Vitamin A for two or three days in children that contract measles. Now Oma's story makes sense."

Grandmother rocked in her chair, caught in her own memories. Anne remained silent, pondering over the lessons contained in Grandmother's story.

"It seems to me," Anne eventually commented, "that our entire life is really about trust. We trust that God loves us in our weaknesses as well as our strengths; trust that He will never abandon us even in our darkest hours; and trust that there is purpose to each experience we have."

"Exactly." Grandmother smiled, pleased that Anne was learning what was important for her heart to heal.

Anne continued thoughtfully. "Our experiences are created from our beliefs, our thoughts and our emotions, which lead to the choices we make. When we look at our results, or our harvest, we learn what works and what doesn't work. Then we can change."

"Yes," Grandmother agreed. "Though remember that some of our experiences are given to us, or we may even have chosen them before we entered mortality, so we could learn."

Anne smiled. "John and I were given a snow storm and a stuck car, and we chose to get in the tractor with George and trust your care for me. Look at all the lessons I have learned in just two days… I see that our choices allow us to learn the difference between pure love and fear, judgment, pride and hate, and the results that each creates."

"In other words," said Grandmother, "these hard parts of our life allow us to learn, through our own experience, the light from the darkness."

Anne stood up and started pacing, caught up in the excitement of her newfound vision of life. "If we fight the painful part of life," she continued, "if we have negative thoughts and emotions about them, we feel we are trapped, like we're sinking into a dark hole with no way out. If, on the other hand, we trust God and let go of feeling like we have to control life, we become open to learning the lessons these experiences have to offer. And we can be grateful for them."

Anne stopped, knelt in front of Grandmother, and held her hands. "Then, as we feel and express gratitude for every part of our lives, we find ourselves riding on top of the waves of life rather than letting them crash on us. We can't avoid the hardships of life, but we can choose to experience them differently. We truly do have the choice to live in the light!

"Thank you, Grandmother. You have changed my life. I believe I am now ready to thank God for my pain. Will you pray with me?"

Grandmother nodded and slid off the rocking chair, kneeling next to Anne.

"Heavenly Father, I give thanks in all things, the bad along with the good. I am thankful for the neck pain and back pain and shoulder pain and leg pain. I am thankful for the allergies and reactions to medications. I am thankful for the stomach pain and diarrhea every time I eat. I am thankful for the depression and anxiety that I so often experience. I am thankful that my children have to live with a mother that doesn't have the energy to play with them. I don't know why they have to live with a sick mother, but I now choose to be thankful for it. I am thankful that my husband chooses to live with a wife that usually can't fix his dinner or iron his clothes. I am thankful that I never know from day to day if I am going to be able to do any work or not. I am thankful for all the people who think I am just a hypochondriac, or who think I am crazy or just lazy.

"It feels strange to me to thank you for these things, God, but now I see purpose in some of the things that have happened to me. I am thankful we got stuck in the snow, and that I got so sick from the cold. These experiences allowed me to be with Grandmother and to learn about myself. I was disheartened and frightened at being sick again, but I see now what a blessing it has been. Please give me faith to be thankful for the difficult experiences that I do not yet understand.

"I say these words in Jesus' name, Amen."

"You have learned well, Anne," smiled Grandmother, tears in her eyes, as she slipped back into her rocking chair. "You have an astute mind, an open heart, and a powerful spirit. I have been truly blessed to be with you these past few days. You are now on the path to healing. I will miss you."

"And I will certainly miss you, Grandmother." Anne bent over, pulling Grandmother close into a long hug. As she stood back up, she glanced out the window. "Oh, dear. I see John coming up the front walk. I was expecting to have you tell me the next Dream Picture. You have one for gratitude, I'm sure."

"Yes, Anne, there is a Dream Picture for gratitude. Open the door for John... John, you came just in time!"

"What, were you ready to throw Anne out the door if I came any later?" he laughed as he stomped the snow off of his feet.

"I've thought about it," chuckled Grandmother, "but Anne has convinced me to do one more Dream Picture for her, and we'd love for you to join us."

"Well, we've got a couple more hours to drive," John said, trying to put on a serious face, "and we've got a car full of that great fresh-from-the-cow milk, homemade jam, and lots of other food. You would think we were June's long-lost relatives, the way she carried on about our leaving." John laughed heartily.

"Oh, John, I know you're teasing me," said Anne. "We've got plenty of time, and the car will be a refrigerator for the food in no time, it's so cold out there. Come sit next to me and enjoy what Grandmother has in store for us."

"Yes, surely you can stay another thirty minutes," said Grandmother. "It will be good for both of you to experience trust and gratitude for all that life has to offer."

*　　*　　*

Make yourself comfortable and listen to the Dream Picture for Chapter 6 on Track 3 of CD 2.

EPILOGUE

From the air-conditioned tractor cab, George watched the plume of dust approaching him, rising between the patchwork of newly plowed ebony fields. He knew it was June's car coming over the rise of the hill. June was visiting the fields more often since their youngest children were in high school and Tyler in college. With George Jr. and Michelle off and married, June had a little extra time on her hands. George was glad. June would often bring a picnic lunch, and they would eat together by the stream in the hollow located in the hills above their mountain valley farm. It was a pretty place of wild green and scattered daisies, and George treasured these times alone with his wife. With the time-consuming work of the farm and a pack of kids, George realized that in almost thirty years of marriage, he had had precious little private time with his sweetheart. His heart picked up every time he saw the plume of dust headed his way.

George climbed down from the cab as June emerged from the car, jumping up and down and waving at him. June seemed extra excited today. George searched his memory to see if he had forgotten that this was an important day. It wasn't their anniversary; that was next month. It wasn't her birthday; that was sometime in the winter. George couldn't come up with anything. He relaxed and started for the car.

"Hurry, George," June shouted. George's long legs were striding along newly plowed rows of fresh smelling topsoil. He picked up his pace.

"What's got you so worked up today?" George asked as he reached the end of the field and hopped over the irrigation ditch.

"I've got a surprise for you!" June exclaimed. "Get in the car, and we'll go over to the hollow so I can tell you. I fixed your favorite picnic: meat-loaf sandwich and pork and beans." She got back in the car. "I had a hard time waiting to come over here after the mailman came."

"So I take it the surprise came in the mail," said George, tucking his long legs into the small car.

"Yes, it did. We got a letter from Anne Carter. Oh, dear, now I've spilled the beans, and it won't be a surprise."

George laughed, cocking his head towards the back seat. "I believe the beans are still safe and sound in the picnic basket."

At the end of the road, the pair followed an overgrown trail to the hollow. George stopped and motioned for June to look. Just above the hollow, a gurgling spring opened into a small pool, made larger by a beaver den that had been there as long as anyone could remember. The emerald pool was surrounded by thickets of willow bushes and was difficult to approach, but the couple could see three beaver kits chasing each other through the water. They were able to watch the kits play for a few minutes before the little balls of fur detected the humans and disappeared.

The richness of the hollow was adorned with emeralds of dew after the recent spring rains. A small stream tumbled over the sticks and logs of the beaver dam and gaily entered the hollow, a grassy area embroidered at the edges with Queen Anne's Lace, with just enough room for a blanket. This was where June and George Woodbury had brought their young children to splash in the stream on hot summer days, and it was where they now found new joy in being a couple.

George spread the well-used patchwork quilt under the ancient oak tree and June set out the inviting picnic meal. After a simple blessing on the food, George picked up a sandwich and smiled at June expectantly. "All right, June, let's hear about Anne's letter."

June pulled out a thick manila envelope. "It's much more than a letter. I'm so excited to tell you! You know we haven't heard from Anne since she came back for Grandmother's funeral over a year ago. I was out pulling weeds in the garden when Fred pulled up with the mail. You remember that Fred's wife has been ailing, so I hurried down the lane to find out how she was doing. I had been thinking of bringing over some fresh-baked bread and some of my special raspberry jam, but since he was there, I asked if he could wait a minute and I could bring it out to him, and…"

"Dagnab it, woman," George interrupted teasingly, "skip the rest of the morning and get to the letter. You could go on all day."

"Well, anyway, Fred winked when he gave me this package. He always winks at me if he knows the mail contains something good. The envelope had Anne's return address on it so you know I couldn't wait to open it. I hurried back to the house and opened it. And guess what was in it?"

"I don't know," said George dryly. "That's why you're going to tell me."

"Well, I won't tell you if you're going to act that way." June folded her arms and pretended to be mad, but her twinkling eyes gave her away, and a smile followed. "Actually, I'm going to let Anne tell you. Here's her letter."

George took the letter from June and unfolded it, recognizing the beautiful script of Anne Carter.

Dear June and George,

First, I must apologize for the length of time between letters. Life has been so busy with John's promotion and all of the children's activities that I haven't taken the time to stay in touch.

We are all happy and doing well. Tina, now fifteen, is still my responsible one. With all of her high school activities and friends, it's good I don't need to depend on her so often anymore. Eric, thirteen, is struggling in school because he doesn't focus well in the subjects he doesn't like. He doesn't like to sit very long to do his homework. We are doing a little home schooling with him, and have worked things out with his teachers, because we feel it is important that he not feel like a failure during this self-discovery time of life. We teach him the lessons of Running Wolf, that his weaknesses are simply blessings from God to help him learn the lessons of life, and we concentrate more on developing his strengths rather than changing his weaknesses. He seems to be happy and well-adjusted.

Rachel, our daughter who was diagnosed with autism, is our little miracle. We have been led to excellent resources, and with various and extensive therapies she has progressed rapidly. She's ten now and is able to go to school with the normal children of her own age group. Even though she continues to have a few peculiar behaviors, most people would never know that she has had any difficulties.

John received a promotion about six months ago, his second in two years. The new job means that he works more hours, but with my health so much improved we are both able to handle the extra hours. As you know, he started a garden three years ago, inspired by you, George. He loves to go out and get his hands in the soil. It seems to relieve the stress of the day for him. When he was working longer hours, I took over some of his garden work, and now I also am hooked on dirty hands. We have yet to get livestock, though John would love to figure out a way to keep a good milking cow in the suburbs.

With some of the extra income from John's promotion, I have hired a part-time housekeeper, and I've been doing something I've never before dreamed of doing. I've been writing a book! When I came back and visited Grandmother the summer after the infamous snowstorm, I convinced her to tell all her stories and Dream Pictures while I recorded them on tape. I used the tapes often with my own family, and my children responded well to them. I listened to the Dream Pictures over and over again as I was going through the process of my own healing. But as I healed and the children grew, the tapes were set aside.

When I received news of Grandmother's death, I remembered the tapes and was so glad that I had her voice and her stories to keep a piece of her alive in my heart. But when I came to her funeral and listened to her loved ones talk about her abundant life, it was as if she sat next to me, whispering in my ear, "Share my stories." I felt her words deep in my heart. "Share my stories, and bring love and healing to the world." This frightened me. I've never written before. It took all my time to simply care for my family. How could I even think I had the capacity to heal the world? But the words were strong, and they stayed with me even after I returned home. So I got out Grandmother's tapes and listened to them again and again. I decided to write my own story, and included the stories that Grandmother told me while I was with her. It took a lot of time and effort, and a lot of ideas and editing from friends and family, but I did it! I found that I could not replace Grandmother telling the Dream Pictures, so I just converted her voice from the tapes onto a CD.

So here it is, the book and the CD. I wanted you to have the first copy because you were the ones that brought me to Grandmother. You saved John and me from much more than a winter blizzard, and we are eternally grateful to you both. I'm sure you'll enjoy bringing a part of Grandmother back into your lives, and maybe you would like to share her stories with your grandchildren.

> All my love,
> Anne

George slowly folded the letter and put it back in the envelope.

"And here it is." June handed the book to John. "Here is the book and the CD. I listened to a little of the CD at home, and I cried when I heard Grandmother's voice again."

"I would love to hear it, too," George said wistfully.

June pulled a portable Walkman from her bag. "George, I know you resist modern technology, but my CD player might help you out here."

George tipped his head back and laughed. "As long as you're still my country girl, I can live with big city technology." He flipped through the pages of the book. "Can you believe Grandmother is still doin' her healing? Look at this. Grandmother and Anne, settin' out to heal the world."

George handed the book back to June and lay down on the blanket. "You know, June, I think the plowin' can wait an hour. Read me the first chapter, and then I'd like to hear Grandmother's first Dream Picture again."

George placed his head in June's lap and looked up at the small patch of blue sky. "Look, June, we have a visitor."

June looked up and saw the eagle, gliding in lazy circles above them, finally landing at the top of the old oak tree. A squirrel, disturbed by the eagle, chattered and scampered away towards the beaver pond. June looked at the beauty around her and watched for a moment as the bees danced around the daisies. She felt surrounded by light and love—almost a perfect love. This place had always seemed so familiar, as if she had seen it long before. When was that? She knew she would eventually remember. June opened the book, and soon her gentle voice rose through swaying leaves of the ancient oak as the green world closed around them.